Dune Child

Ella Thorp Ellis

This edition is published by Dune Child Press.
Dune Child was first published by El León Literary Arts.

For information contact:
EllaThorpEllis@gmail.com

Cover designer: Andrea Young
Book designer: Sara Glaser

*El León Literary Arts is a 501c3
nonprofit private foundation established
to extend the array of voices essential
to a democracy's arts and education.*
Publisher: Thomas Farber
Managing editor: Kit Duane
www.elleonliteraryarts.org

ISBN 978-0-692-80021-8
Library of Congress Number 2011923580

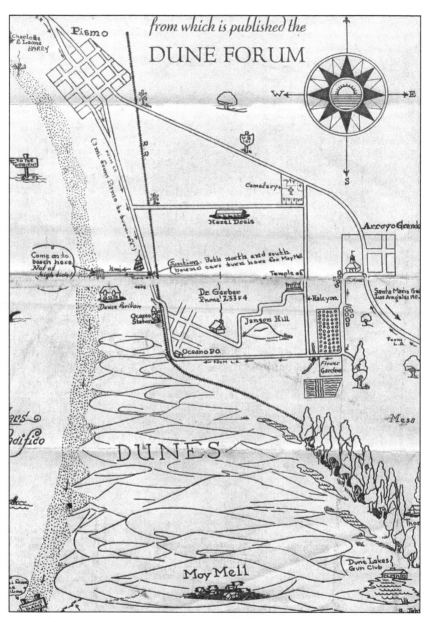

Map of Moy Mell in relation to the surrounding dunes,
Oceano, Pismo, and California Coast.

To my father.

Memories bring back the sound of your voice.

Thank you, Dunham.

Postcard photo of dunes, Oceano, California.
Courtesy of Lesley Gerber Benn.

Preface

WHEN MY MOTHER GOT PREGNANT with me she and my father headed west to Hollywood where he had screen writing contacts. I was born; they got married. He became Joan Crawford's press agent. This was Hollywood in 1931.

Then the Depression shrank movie audiences. Talkies replaced silent films. The movie industry retooled. Joan Crawford quit acting to retrain her squeaky voice. My father lost his job. I got polio at a year and a half.

A poet named Hugo Seelig told us of a beach town up the coast where an osteopathic physician, Dr. Gerber, had remarkable success helping polio children. My father saw this as his chance to take a year off. He would write the great American novel, build a log cabin and raise honeybees. We'd live off the land. My mother would write poetry and play her violin. I would learn to walk again.

We moved to a mesa above the little town of Oceano. My dad built a log cabin. My mother wrote poetry. I got treatments and learned to walk again.

Gavin Arthur, the grandson of President Chester Allen Arthur, asked my father to edit a literary magazine he was publishing in the sand dunes south of Oceano. Gavin expected his *Dune Forum* to be politically progressive and become a major literary voice. We moved to Moy Mell, a dune communal colony of young people in their twenties. Some of the writers, photographers, composers, and spiritual leaders who lived in or visited Moy Mell would later become famous. Meanwhile, they lived on fish, clams, homegrown vegetables, and culls from a vegetable packing shed.

We called ourselves Dunites. I was usually the only child.

CHAPTER

1

W henever I think of home I see myself sitting by the Pacific Ocean at dawn, leaning on a gunnysack full of clams. The year is 1933 and I am four years old.

"Hold the fort, Ella," my father, who had dug the clams, shouts over his shoulder as he drops his pitchfork and disappears into high sand dunes behind us. Then I see the game warden's grey car heading down the beach.

My dad will get five days in jail if he's caught clamming, because he doesn't have a license. No one we know can afford a clamming license since they don't have paying jobs. I don't need a license because I'm a child. The game warden is inching his way along. He's giving my dad time to disappear. It's the Depression and the warden doesn't want to catch Dunites who need the clams to survive.

I look back and my father, Dunham, has disappeared. There are only sand dunes as I lean on the gunnysack of clams. Good, my father's safe. The game warden pulls his Plymouth up behind the high tide line and parks. I wave to him, hugging my sweatshirt around me, and he waves back.

"Looks like you had good diggings this morning, Ella," he says, with a grin.

"Not too bad," I reply as my mother suggests. She says the warden is lucky to have a job in a Depression town where damn few find work so we have to help him go by the rules.

He checks my sack to make sure we haven't taken clams under the legal five inches, rubs my head, and says, "You're not much bigger than a clam, yourself."

My father doesn't come out until the warden's car is far down the beach but then he hoists the gunnysack of clams to his shoulder and we head up the path along a ridge through willows to our home in Moy Mell, where breakfast is waiting. My father, William Dunham Thorp, who prefers that I call him Dunham, is a handsome man with deep-set grey eyes, curly brown hair and a presence that makes people want to hear what he's got to say.

Oceano Beach, our beach, lies halfway up the coast of California, separating the Pacific Ocean from a stretch of live dunes, their sand ground from the Sierra foothills over a thousand years and washed down rivers to our beach and our twenty mile stretch of dunes.

I live with my parents a quarter mile back from the ocean, in an oasis called Moy Mell, Gaelic for land of honey. My father edits the *Dune Forum*. A dozen or more people living with us also work on the magazine. We have three frame houses, two house tents for guests, and a garden in a cove surrounded by dunes and out of the wind. I am the only child living in the colony. The other Moy Mell Dunites are in their twenties and have come to the dunes to write or paint or photograph.

Some of us will be famous one day. This makes us different from the hermits who build driftwood shacks in coves near ours. These men are older and expect less of life. They have been put out of work by the Depression; maybe they've gone hungry. They feel "damn lucky" to have landed in a free spot where they can clam and fish and plant small gardens.

When we hike into town the grocer always says I live in a free-love nudist colony. I can't understand the anger in his voice, because as he says this he is also giving me candy and I know he carries us on credit. Marion, my mother, tells me not to argue, just to tell him we're artists. I do and he rolls his eyes.

THIS MORNING DUNHAM AND I walk home slowly. My legs had been paralyzed by polio when I was eighteen months old and only about half the muscles in each leg function. I lived more than a year strapped into a steel and canvas frame that looked like a gurney. My father and uncle carried me up and down the hill, pretending the gurney I was strapped to was Aladdin's magic carpet.

Still, though trudging through the deep sand strengthens my remaining leg muscles, doctors warn that I must never get tired. So we stop at the top of the willow ridge looking down into Moy Mell. It's my favorite time of the day because I have my father all to myself. Also, Indians once lived in these dunes and we are near one of their shell mounds. I spot a spearhead and dive for it, holding it up proudly.

Ella Thorp Ellis with her father, Dunham Thorp.

"Congratulations, Gooch. Gavin will give you a quarter for a spearhead, more than most of us grown-ups have.

"That's because Gavin is the grandson of President Chester A. Arthur."

"And I'll inherit a barony. Those things don't mean a hell of a lot," Dunham says gently as we stand hand in hand looking down into a willow thicket on one side and a cypress grove on the other. Beyond the coves we see sand and sky, stretching two miles back to the Oceano railroad depot and for nearly twenty miles along the beach. Here and there we can spot other clamshell mounds left by Indian tribes who once dug clams and baked them over fires on these same dunes. Then we turn around and there is the ocean. I inhale, smelling salt and sage and a faint essence of sea creatures.

"There she blows, all the way to China, Gooch." He always says this.

The ocean pulls me like a tide. Surf lulls me to sleep at night and wakes me in the morning. Fish and clams feed us. Seals, sea lions, whales, and the birds are my companions. I grow rich collecting sand dollars. Even today I need to see and breathe the fresh salty fishy smell of the ocean. I need to live where I can hear the surf.

"John and Arther have fires and so does the community house," I say. "I'm getting hungry." I see trails of smoke.

John Doggett and Arther Allman have built driftwood shacks in the small coves to the right of the willows we pass. Doggett is a man in his sixties who bet once too often on the horse races and lost his wife, his house, and his job. He wound up in the dunes, planted a garden, and took up the fiddle.

Arther is an Irishman, well educated and penniless. He ran away to sea. At one point, he says, he was Vice Admiral of the Ecuadorian Navy, until he sank their only gunboat while delivering a twenty-one-gun salute. He was lucky to get out of that country alive.

Dunham and I start down the trail into our cove. I wave to Carl Beckstead, a poet who is milking my goat, Dancer. As soon as my fingers are a little stronger, he'll teach me to milk her. She gives our only milk so it's an important job and I can hardly wait.

We drop the gunnysack of clams by the back door.

"Not bad, Ella. Run into the warden?" Carl asks with a grin.

"She handled him like a pro," Dunham says as Carl finishes milking and carries the milk bucket into the kitchen. Then Carl hands him coffee and me cocoa that he has waiting for us.

My dad wiggles his ears in thanks, which always makes me laugh. Carl hands me honey and mush with goat's milk before he and my father settle down outside the door and begin cleaning the clams, prying them open, washing out sand, and cutting out the valve. They toss the clams in a round grey enamel laundry tub.

Pretty Dolores, Dunham's friend, comes in and is set to peeling potatoes and onions from Carl's garden. The onions smell good but make her cry. Carl has also collected pea and celery rejects from the Oceano railroad packing shed and carried them back over the dunes in gunnysacks for the chowder.

Dunham always says Carl has good poet training because he was born and raised on a potato farm and then went to sea as a commercial fisherman. He's trained to get up in the morning.

Of course, no one gets up as early as my father, who starts writing his novel at four and works until seven. I'm glad Dunham gets up and writes because he wakes me when he's done and we go for our walk, sometimes clamming, sometimes talking as he tells me the names of the plants and birds we see along the way.

"How many for dinner tonight?" Dolores asks, eyeing the tub and giving Dunham a kiss.

He shrugs. "Fifteen. More if Edward Weston gets in and brings family." Edward Weston's photos of our dunes already hang in museums.

I pray Edward won't bring family because then he lets one of his sons go out photographing with him and carry his big square plates. If he comes by himself, I get to carry his plates. I love watching him set up the camera tripod, then screw up his face and consider the shot from different angles, then stand there, and finally bend over the camera and press the shutter. I'm proud when he calls me his little helper and I don't talk so he can concentrate on taking photographs for the world. Interruptions can make him lose a photograph forever.

Marion, my mother, says I might grow up to look at the world like Edward does and I can see this pleases her.

My mother sleeps until noon, which Dunham says is apparently her poet's rhythm. Not Carl's. We're morning people. That's when my father calls me his Gooch and makes pancakes in the shape of my age and name.

I have been reading *Billy Whiskers* to him and Pretty Dolores and Carl. I'm learning to read and am thrilled to share the story of the high-spirited goat who got into even more trouble than our goat, Dancer. Dunham and I have read together since I had polio and we'd go through the Sears Roebuck catalogue, picking out all the things I'd be able to use when I could walk again.

Everyone talks in the morning. Then, after breakfast, the grown-ups go off by themselves to write or edit *Dune Forum* articles. *Time* magazine wrote that they agreed with our publisher that the *Dune Forum* would be a force shifting literary thought from the East to the West Coast so everyone's trying hard. In the afternoon most people meditate or read. Those who get up late, like my mother, do their writing or painting. Dunham revises what he's written in the morning on his novel. Sometimes he'll get into arguments about the Depression and can't be interrupted. However, once or twice a week when the tide is right and it isn't too cold, Dunham and Marion and I go for a swim in the afternoon.

The three of us head for the beach hand in hand. This is the only time, except in bed, that my mother doesn't wear glasses, and she's beautiful without them. I always walk between my parents so they'll swing me high off the sand. I love how the salty fishy smell of the ocean intensifies once we climb over that last dune to the beach.

"What's it going to be today, Ella, backstroke or sidestroke?"

I consider. "Backstroke, please." I like lying on my back and looking up at the sky, watching the gulls and pelicans riding the wind currents. Putting my nose in the water chokes me. I can't breathe.

"Okay, we'll start with backstroke and do a little sidestroke at the end. Right?"

I nod. "You always say that."

We're wading into the cold surf. Marion and I get goose pimples. Dunham dives right into the first good-sized wave and comes out kicking. My mother lifts me with both arms so the water only comes to my waist.

"Coney Island is a lot warmer," she says.

"Not bad at all once you get wet, Marion."

We're in the calm water between the breakers and the big waves. I lie back on my small inner tube, kicking and backstroking for all I'm worth to keep from freezing. Dunham circles back to me, and Marion heads into deep water for a swim. She won swimming contests in high school and I love to watch her.

There is something else. My father and I have her complete attention. She is with us, focused on us, not daydreaming or reading, not sleeping or thinking out loud, not talking to someone else. She circles back to us now just as one of the big breakers lifts my inner tube and me. The water lifts me high and passes under me, then under Dunham, in what my mother calls our private roller coaster.

Then she and Dunham have me swim backstroke between them, all three of us laughing.

"Good work. Now, a few sidestrokes, Ella."

I stiffen. Suddenly, I'm cold again. My father takes off for a swim and Marion holds me so I can still breathe and I sidestroke. It's all right so long as her arms are around me, holding me safe.

Then we're back on the beach toweling ourselves off and slipping into sweatshirts. I always love going back across the dunes because my father hoists me to his shoulders, he and my mother hold hands, and we sing all the way home.

Usually.

On this particular day, we are drying each other off when Dunham begins to wave at a car coming down the beach.

"It's Upton Sinclair," he says with a big smile. "I've been wanting to talk with him."

I groan but he pays no attention.

Upton Sinclair has written about the evils of our system, which over-produces things people haven't the money to buy. He and Dunham say that's why we're in a Depression. Marion says he loves Moy Mell because we've made a good life for ourselves by helping each other. He and my father think communism is another form of imperialism but socialism is good because it means sharing. Everyone we know votes Democratic. I won't even meet a Republican until I'm in fifth grade and we've moved.

My mother likes socialism because then everyone will have enough to eat and a place to live and a lot of people don't have either of these in 1933. The only thing I don't like about socialism is Upton Sinclair, who comes to talk with my father and doesn't like a kid who butts in. My dad always blames me for interrupting, not Upton Sinclair.

"Marion?" My father speaks in what Marion calls his imperial voice,

"Dunham, would you like Ella and me to go on ahead so you two can talk?"

I groan but my father smiles at Marion as she takes my hand and we head across the beach toward Moy Mell.

"Never mind, Baby. They share ideas and it helps to hear them in this disappointing world."

I refuse to sing.

I hate Upton Sinclair.

CHAPTER

2

Edward Weston didn't come for dinner that night. There was no telephone so my father and Gavin would have to find another photographer to do the cover for the next *Dune Forum*. Fortunately, Gavin ran into Ansel Adams climbing over the dunes and he did a study of two anchors for our cover.

Gavin, a historian turned astrologer, founded *Dune Forum* with money he'd inherited from his grandfather, Chester A. Arthur, a U.S. president. Gavin hoped the magazine would become the literary voice of the West Coast. *Time* magazine quoted him saying the magazine might replace Eastern literary thought. In the depths of the Depression, which prevented many talented writers from selling, he was able to form a gifted *Dune Forum* staff and get celebrities to contribute articles, poems, and photos. He was also a personal friend of President Franklin Roosevelt, who founded the New Deal.

Gavin Arthur, publisher of Dune Forum *and grandson of President Chester A. Arthur.*
Courtesy of Dr. R. W. Gerber Family Papers.

"My friend Franklin says—" he would begin, reducing any room to silence.

Our cove was protected on the windward side by a eucalyptus and a cypress grove, which kept shifting sand from covering our houses. The smaller houses had wood stoves; the community house also had a stove that used bottled gas. Each house had a fireplace, and walls of books, many of them from the President's library. None had electricity, running water, or plumbing. We all used the same outhouse, the same well, ate fish and clams from the ocean and vegetables from our gardens. Gavin shared cooking dinners with my father. Everyone met for dinner at the big community house table or outside around a bonfire.

As Gavin heard of people he wanted for *Dune Forum* and our community he would invite them, as he'd invited us. Some visited, some stayed. Carl had been there longest and kept the garden, goat, and houses in working order but no one would have thought of calling him a caretaker. He was a poet.

Both community and *Dune Forum* work had to be on a no-cash communal basis. 1933 was a deep Depression year. Gavin's inheritance had been depleted by the magazine, and before that, by the fight for Irish Independence. His motto was "individualism within community," which meant sharing the work as well as the thinking. He had a theory that each era of history was linked to the precession of the equinox and spanned 720 years. He also communed with the spirits of the Chumash Indians who had lived where we did and died there a hundred years before we arrived.

His comings and goings were curious and mysterious to me. I felt betrayed once when I heard him laugh and tell Upton Sinclair, who didn't like me, that I was "a clever little spy." Gavin's laughter hurt but he was right. I did spy on him. Of course. Among other things, I'd heard grown-ups say he was bisexual and, though I had no idea what that meant, I got the idea that this was part of what made Gavin so special. His relationships with his first wife Charlotte, and with two men and a woman he took into his house, fascinated me. He and his friends laughed, kissed, and talked more animatedly together than anyone else I knew.

I also loved to watch the guests he brought to Moy Mell, some of whom Gavin later forgot he'd invited and who hiked in when he was away, famous people who needed clean sheets and could only drink good wine. We kept clean sheets on hand for such emergencies. As my mother said, every night was party time with Gavin and we counted on resting when he was gone.

And I counted on Gavin's many small kindnesses, such as paying me a dime for every Indian arrowhead I found and a quarter each for the rare spearheads the wind uncovered in the sand. This was the only money I remember having until I was about eight years old and learned to weed.

WE OFTEN CARRIED OUR SUPPER out onto the dunes and ate around a bonfire under the stars, talking and singing far into the night—the smells of sage and a salty sea, the sound of the surf mellowing us. If I fell asleep Dunham would carry me in to bed. If I stayed awake Marion would take me on her lap and sing to me.

One night I particularly remember we had two dancers visiting from New York, Muriel and Paul Draper. They were wearing Greek togas and Muriel had a diaphanous yellow shawl. They danced by fire and moon light, dipping and whirling, the first classical modern dance I had seen. They seemed to float over the dunes, the moon rising behind them highlighting Indian shell mounds and the faces around the fire, the rapt faces of people who loved me. My mother and father sat on either side of me, holding hands.

I watched in ecstasy! The dancers were so beautiful. They seemed the spirit of life itself. Maybe I wouldn't be a photographer when I grew up. I could be a dancer and float over the dunes like Muriel. There was my polio, of course. I could walk but not run and, at best, I trudged through the deep sand. Sometimes when I was tired, I had to crawl. But there was time yet. I was barely five. I'd practice.

THE NEXT MORNING, STILL UNDER the spell of the dance, I climbed over the willow ridge dividing Moy Mell from the coves where Arther Allman and John Doggett lived, eager to tell them about becoming a dancer.

What luck! They were sitting in the sun before Arther's South Sea Island shack. Arther was puffing his broken pipe while whittling on one of his Indonesian lady heads, his hand curved around his old black-handled jackknife, his stubby fingers stained red, blue, and yellow from the native plant dyes he used to color his statues. He also tried the dye out on his grey hair so he had strips of red, yellow, and blue hair too. He worked quickly on the driftwood, and the eyes, nose and mouth were roughed in by the time I made it through the willows, avoiding the poison oak, and presented myself.

Arther, who'd been all over the world after he ran away to sea and told even better stories than Gavin, was my closest friend.

But John Doggett, at the moment drinking coffee and rolling his day's supply of cigarettes, was great, too. He was—as my mother Marion had said more than once—a man who had bet on the horses once too often. How he found his way to the dunes with his fiddle intact, she couldn't

Arther Allman's South Sea Island shack.
Allman's fellow Dunite, George Blaiz, stands in front.
Courtesy of Dr. R. W. Gerber Family Papers.

imagine. By the time we arrived in Moy Mell he had managed to build a warm driftwood house with a tarpaper roof and to plant a thriving garden. He planted daffodils for me.

"Guess what? I'm going to be a dancer when I grow up."

"All right," Doggett said.

"Like Muriel Draper?" Arther asked, with his usual perception, putting aside carving his Indonesian lady's head and getting up to fix me a cup of cocoa. His wood stove and his kitchen implements were outside, dishes and staples set up in a series of apple crates so he could enjoy the sun and the sand and the stars. He did move most of his things inside for the winter.

"Well, Ella my girl, here's to dancing over the dunes in a few years," Arther said, clicking his cup of cowboy coffee against my mug of cocoa. Doggett brought out his fiddle to celebrate.

ONE NIGHT SOON AFTER THIS we were again having supper by a bonfire. There were no guests. Gavin had managed to get his car across the creek and was taking *Dune Forum* to the printer in San Francisco. The Moy

Mell regulars were relaxed and sitting easy. Carl read a few poems. Marion took out her violin. Dunham had just asked, as he often did, if she'd give "Moonlight Sonata" a try. My mother played well and the lovely opening notes sent shivers down my spine. My father looked peaceful and happy. There was a light breeze.

Then the call of the coyotes echoed from dune to dune. I looked up to find out where they were and, instead, saw Edward Weston walking in over the moonlit dunes with his camera and tripod over one shoulder.

"Hooray!" He was alone, which meant I could carry his photographic plates for him tomorrow morning. I stopped, my mouth open, surprised at myself. How could I have thought—even for a week—that I might want to be a dancer rather than a photographer?

THE NEXT MORNING EDWARD and I started out soon after sunrise, when the dunes were still damp and dark, the surf up by the sound of it. He was quiet and so was I because he'd explained that he had to concentrate in order to catch the best photographic moment, the image he'd lose forever if he didn't focus. And the world would be poorer for not having that photograph. I was trying to remember his words so I could repeat them to Marion, who would explain what he meant. It was enough that he talked to me as if I were a grown-up. More than enough.

We trudged on and on. How could he carry that heavy tripod and camera through the deep sand? Did I dare ask to rest when he was concentrating? Suppose he missed his chance to help the world and it was all my fault? My legs hurt but we kept walking, up and down and up again, trudging through the sand.

Finally he stopped and set up the tripod, fussed with the camera and asked for a plate. I handed him one and gratefully sat down. I sighed. He rubbed the top of my head. Then Edward seemed to stalk the camera, looking at the windblown patterns etched into the sand of the great dune before us from every angle and from different heights. Finally he snapped a picture. He took several plates of the one dune. He took his time and I was getting sleepy when he finally straightened up and smiled.

"All right, I think I've got her. Let's head back for breakfast."

"The photo for the world?"

"For the world, yes, but *Dune Forum* gets first crack at it."

"Can I tell Dunham?"

Edward gave me that look grown-ups did when they realized I called my parents by their first names. This was confusing. I always used their names and they wanted me to. When I asked Marion why grown-ups seemed surprised, she said it was new to them and they'd get used to it. It was just part of making the world a fairer and friendlier place for us all, in her opinion.

IT HAD BEEN RAINING STEADILY for a week when it came time to take *Dune Forum* with Edward's dune photo for the cover to the printer. Dunham was taking this edition up and he and I walked the beach and checked the creek daily. He had to drive our Ford coupe, Belinda, across that creek and on up the coast to San Francisco. The rain stopped in the nick of time. The tides tamed and the creek level began to recede a little. Carl would go with Dunham until he'd crossed the creek, just in case, because Carl was our towing expert. Sometimes he even earned cash pulling cars out when they got stuck in the sand or the creek.

"Would you like to come along and walk back with Carl?"

"More than anything in the whole world."

"I hope you're exaggerating."

We both laughed.

The sand was packed hard by the rains and we sped over the beach, scattering colonies of gulls and sandpipers in our wake. We ran over long ropes of seaweed, popping the pods. It was low tide. My father would cross at the mouth of the creek where it was shallow. But waves were high today. Dunham turned off the engine and considered. He needed to hit the creek at just the right moment, between waves. He turned on the ignition, still waiting. Finally he revved the engine and plunged in. A large wave suddenly rolled in out of nowhere and flooded us, even splashing over our windshield. After it passed Dunham tried to start the engine again. No luck.

"Damn it to hell."

Dunham never swore. I shivered.

Carl tried to start the engine while Dunham carried the *Dune Forum* manuscript, wrapped in oil paper and still dry, to safety. I had to sit on the bank beside Dunham's suitcase, jacket, and the manuscript. I sat there freezing all afternoon while Dunham and Carl struggled with the car. The tide rose and finally they had to abandon Belinda. They'd come back the next day and pull her out. But the rains pelted us and it was four days before they could divert the creek and pull Belinda loose with a borrowed truck. Then they hooked our car to the back of the truck.

"Carl's walking back to Moy Mell. Want to go with him or come on to Halcyon with me and the car, Gooch?"

"What's Halcyon?" I asked as I climbed up into the seat next to my father.

"Tell Marion Ella's safe with me at the Varians' and I'll send her back in a few days."

We both waved goodbye.

"HALCYON IS A THEOSOPHIST COMMUNITY built around a big white octagon temple," Dunham began. As we rode up the beach, through the town of Oceano, he told me about Halcyon, where people lived because they were Theosophists. They believed in Jesus and seven reincarnations and loving one another. We were going to Halcyon because a friend of Dunham's who lived there was an inventor, a mechanical genius, and had offered to get the car running.

"Is the temple like where the Wizard of Oz lived?" Marion had been reading me Dorothy's adventures in Oz.

"What made you ask that, Ella? Actually, L. Frank Baum, who wrote the *Wizard of Oz*, was a Theosophist."

We were driving through fragrant blooming apricot orchards, wet sand still shaking off the Ford coupe behind our truck. Then I saw the sun shining on the octagonal white stone temple with lines so simple and so different from any other building I'd ever seen that it didn't look built but as if sculpted and appearing by magic.

Fields of California poppies stretched down the slope to nearby houses, each surrounded by blooming gardens. The poppies blooming in drifts down from the temple made it so easy to see Dorothy and the Cowardly Lion and Tin Man stumbling sleepily through these fields.

My father pulled into a driveway leading up to a big Victorian house and yet another garden.

"We're here. The Varian place," he said and switched off the engine.

I climbed down from the truck and looked around.

Coming down the steps was a big bear of a man, maybe the tallest man I'd ever seen. He grinned at me and held out his hands. "I'm Russ Varian, and who are you?"

"I'm Ella and this is my father."

"Dunham and I are old friends."

I spent most of the next five days in the Varian garage, sitting on a stool while Dunham and Russ took Belinda's engine apart, wiped off every piece in clean water and set it out to dry. When the engine part was dry, Russ

A cover of Dune Forum, published by Gavin Arthur and edited by Dunham Thorp.

wiped it carefully with oil and reinserted it into the engine chassis—pistons, valves, screws—Russ told me the names of each part and I forgot most of them. If I got tired or bored I ran outside and played with the half dozen Varian cats.

A FEW YEARS LATER, in Palo Alto, my father and I watched Russ and his brother Sig working with early television, when there was still nothing but light and dots on the screen. At that time they were also working on the Klystron tube, which would become such a crucial part of radar and save many lives in World War II.

Finally, Belinda was working well enough to haul the magazine on to San Francisco. Unfortunately, magazines that cost thirty cents and hit the newsstands two weeks late in the depths of the Depression didn't sell well, no matter how good they were. Looking back on it years later, Dunham said that *Dune Forum* was probably doomed at the moment that first wave poured in over Belinda. Of course, no one thought so at the time.

CHAPTER

3

That summer of 1933 I turned five. On the night before my birthday a medium sized black and white stray dog followed my father home over the dunes from town and became my dog. Dribbly, named after a dribble of white spots down his throat and chest, loved everyone but he loved Dunham and me the most. He followed us everywhere, tail wagging, and soon even the coyotes accepted him. Our goat, Dancer, also black and white and only a little bigger, apparently thought Dribbly was her kid. At least that's how my mother explained why Dancer herded and licked the dog. They often slept curled up together. Sometimes I'd curl up and nap with them.

"It comes down to the fact that Dancer's a bossy goat and Dribbly's a patient dog," my father said, smiling at my mother.

That was the same summer Arther Allman began to write and illustrate his book *The Lost Continent of Atlantis*. Everyone in Moy Mell did their own writing or painting or photography as well as their work to get Gavin's magazine out. My father and Gavin were writing novels. My mother wrote poetry. Carl sold cowboy stories to the pulp magazines. Carl's girlfriend, Mary-who-could-do-anything, earned what little cash we had by sending in episodes for the radio soap opera *Our Gal Sunday*. John Steinbeck came by and read us chapters from his manuscript, *Tortilla Flat*. Edward Weston, Willard Van Dyke, and Ansel Adams were photographing every dune in sight. The arts were in the air. So it wasn't surprising that the older Dunites, spread out in driftwood shacks across the dunes, also began writing and painting.

A year or two later this creative drive in the dunes inspired my father's utopian theory, based on the belief that if people worked to earn a living four hours a day and devoted another four to creative work, including child rearing and cooking, it would solve the growing problem of an excess work force and create a more peaceful and satisfying world.

But the world in Arther's manuscript was far from peaceful. He had pen and ink illustrations that made my hair stand on end. He drew horned dev-ils and goblins with tails and wings who cavorted on every page. He drew lost souls living on a lost continent. He even put my goat, Dancer, into his manuscript one afternoon after she knocked over his stew. He called her the demon goat and soon he was drawing a herd of demon goats.

"What's a sculptor doing writing a novel?" Marion asked him after I told her I was having bad dreams about Arther's demons and goblins.

Arther scratched himself all over, thinking. "Seemed time," he said finally.

The only other person I knew who saw devils and goblins was Aussie Slim, the drunk who lived in a shack out by the beach with a roof made of clamshells and windows made of car windshields. He was dirty and shook and twitched and muttered. He clenched his fists and hit out at me or anyone else within range. Marion said "poor Slim" got delirium tremens and that was what made him see devils. He lived out by the beach because he could find liquor bottles washed in by the tide. Sometimes the bottles hadn't even been opened and my father thought bootleggers left them so Slim wouldn't tell the game warden he'd seen them. Carl said that on a bad day when all the bottles were empty Slim would line them up and spark a cigarette lighter to the bottom of a bottle until the heat drew the residue from the sides and bottom and Slim could get a good swallow from each bottle. I always wanted to watch this but Slim terrified me and I was afraid to get close enough to ask.

Arther didn't shake or twitch. He wasn't drunk. He was my friend. Yet here he was, sitting in the sun, leaning against his cabin, drawing these terrible goblins and devils, and all the time he had this happy smile on his face. He couldn't bear Slim so he didn't get the goblins and demons from him.

"Where did you get them? And where was this Atlantis continent lost from?"

"Continental drift maybe. Ella, I'm just making up a story. With a story, you can read it or not, just suit yourself," he said. "In twenty years you might enjoy this. I'm not writing for children."

"But it scares me. Like Slim does."

"Then forget it. Just say demons are Arther's cup of tea. Okay?"

SO I WENT HUNTING for Marion. She'd know about Atlantis. She got up about noon and "did so enjoy" a first cup of coffee in bed. My father, mother, and I had the bedroom behind the community house kitchen so it wasn't too far to carry coffee. It was already made—from fresh well water—and I put a can of it on the wood stove. When it was heated up, I poured it carefully into a cup, but even so I spilled some. Wiping it up I remembered that Carl and I were going to wash and refill the kerosene lamps that afternoon. Cleaning, refilling, and trimming wicks on kerosene lamps with Carl was special because he told me stories while we worked.

I found my mother, Marion, lying in bed staring up at the ceiling. Just staring. She didn't see me come in. She didn't answer when I said hello. She just stared up at the ceiling. This happened sometimes lately. It was creepy. I felt as if I'd lost my mother. She'd left me forever, even though I could see her, lying right there in her own bed.

"I brought you coffee." I yelled because I wanted her to stop looking so spooky. There was a long moment and then her eyes turned toward me and came alive again. She reached out to hug me and smiled as I put down the coffee. Marion was back, my mother again. She rummaged around for tobacco and asked me to roll her a cigarette.

She lit her cigarette and took a long drag, blowing smoke rings into the air for me. We both giggled.

"What's bothering you?" she asked, taking my hand.

"It's Arther. Why is he writing—THAT—book?"

"Ah, it's the Irish in him. The runaway imagination, all that energy. Lord help them, my uncles back in Brooklyn were just the same."

"They wrote about devils?"

"No, but they kept goats and they taught every one of us children to play the violin."

"Arther made Dancer a demon goat in his book."

"Ah, immortality! Lucky Dancer."

"I hate devils. And Dancer is no demon goat."

"But Arther's devils are more like—elves. And it's an honor to be in a book."

I thought that over while Marion began to dress. We could both hear Dunham talking with Upton Sinclair out on the kitchen stoop, my father's voice soft and respectful, Upton Sinclair's loud and sure. Even the good smell of oatmeal cookies baking didn't make up for that. She doesn't really like him, either, I thought, looking at Marion's sad face. But I didn't ask. My mother would never say a word against Sinclair because he was such a good and famous socialist and a writer whose novels helped the world. Marion was a great believer in good.

"Arther asked me to come over for lunch," I lied. Better Arther and his goblins than being seen but not heard with Upton Sinclair doing all the talking.

Marion nodded absently and I was free to run down into the willows where no one could see me and I could overhear what Dunham and Upton Sinclair were saying. I circled back around the community house to where the willows began and crawled underneath, shimmying my way over toward where my father and my enemy sat in the sun. I loved this spot, loved the damp fresh smell of willows, loved the game of spying.

"I might just consider a run for governor next year—on the Democratic ticket, of course. The Democrats in the legislature—and in Hollywood—have been urging me to. They think I can beat Frank Merriam."

Dunham took a long drag on his cigarette and then said, "Good, you'll pull California out of the Depression, if anyone can."

"And you'll come with me, Dunham. We'll stump the state and you'll see we get coverage in the papers," Upton Sinclair said. "My wife is afraid the movie studios and the newspapers will gang up on me. Back the big farm monopolies."

My father knew about press releases because he'd been a press agent before Gavin asked him to be his editor for *Dune Forum* and we moved to Moy Mell.

"How long at a time would I be away from Moy Mell, Upton?"

Away? I gasped so loudly that both men looked up. Luckily neither saw me.

Sinclair shrugged and muttered something I couldn't hear.

Dunham Thorp (center) discussing Upton Sinclair's campaign for governor of California in 1934. At far left is Ella's dog, Dribbly.
Courtesy of Dr. R. W. Gerber Family Papers.

Dunham frowned. "A lot depends on *Dune Forum*. Gavin depends on me and he's been a good friend," he said, finally.

I'd have to live with Upton Sinclair? Every day?

"Surely the Democratic Party and our EPIC platform mean more to the state of California than a failing literary magazine."

I remember the haunted look that settled on my father's face. The word *failure* was no joke in Depression days. His expression scared me so that I stumbled and fell through the willows right at their feet.

"No, no, no, no! We can't leave Moy Mell," I gasped as my father helped me up.

"Just give us a moment, Ella," he said, as he looked me over for scratches.

"Spying again, Ella? Impossible child. Scoot! We're talking."

Upton Sinclair and I stared at each other.

"He's my father," I told him.

He turned his back on me.

"Just a few minutes, Gooch," Dunham said, gently giving me a little push on the back.

I gave my father a hurt look and stalked around them into the kitchen, where I could still hear what they were saying.

"Gavin's in Santa Barbara now, raising money. You know I'd like nothing better than campaigning with you," Dunham said, lighting another cigarette. "But I have a family. My wife isn't very strong these days."

"Leave them here. We can subsidize food and clothing for them. This is your chance to make a difference for California, probably for the whole country."

"Let me think about it?"

They stood up and shook hands. I was trembling. My own father was thinking of abandoning me and going off with Mr. Grumpy. I told Dunham I was going to Arther's for lunch.

"Have a good time," he said. He didn't care. Upton Sinclair frowned.

I scooted back under the willows, scratching myself, and finally came out at the path to Arther's. I told him only that Sinclair was thinking of running for governor, which Arther thought was the best news he'd heard all day. Arther put his demon illustrations away and I stayed for curry and half a Hershey bar and only went back when I heard people walking along the willow ridge toward the beach.

"You missed Upton but you're in time to help clean the kerosene lamps," Carl said with a grin. He knew how I felt.

I shrugged and helped Carl and Pretty Dolores clear the table. Everyone else had walked out to the beach to say goodbye to Sinclair and collect driftwood for the night's fire and, as Carl said, to settle the world's affairs. Laughter drifted back and I relaxed. I began to collect the kerosene lamps and line them up on the big community house table. Carl brought in a can of kerosene and the wick roll.

"Time for a story?" I asked as Carl sat down and began taking out the glass chimneys and washing them in the soapy warm bucket of water Dolores brought in before she went off to meditate. Dolores was a Basque from Spain and a Buddhist so she had to meditate every afternoon.

I yearned to get old enough so Carl would trust me to wash the delicate glass chimneys. Maybe when you're seven, he always said. Dribbly slept on my feet and Carl told me a story of when he was five and lived on a potato farm in Bakersfield.

By the time the others came back from the beach loaded with driftwood I'd almost forgotten the Upton Sinclair conversation. It was only a bad dream.

Moy Mell: Community House (left) and Gavin's house (right).
Courtesy of Dr. R. W. Gerber Family Papers.

CHAPTER

4

*F*all 1933

One balmy August evening my father and I climbed back over the dunes
after seeing my mother and the other Moy Mell people off on a trek to
Santa Barbara to lay in quilts and clothes from the Goodwill and Salvation
Army stores. Dunham had stayed home to get some writing done and look
after me. Besides, he said he'd rather go naked than wear leftovers. Back in
the cove we found our friend Carl in what he called a great blue funk.

"I'm at the end of my rope," Carl said. "How in hell am I going to get
through another winter stone broke in the sand dunes? Indians who lived
in these dunes a hundred years ago are beginning to haunt me.

"If I don't eat a steak pretty soon I'll go out of my mind," he added,
taking a deep draw on his cigarette, when Dunham and I were silent. "I'm
beginning to hate clams, I'm sick of fish, and I never did like vegetables
much. More fun to grow them than eat the pithy old things. Didn't you

and Gavin come up with *Dune Forum* to jolt us out of this damn Depression, Dunham?"

"Takes time." My father looked sad.

"But didn't you and Gavin turn socialist to help us ordinary folk?"

"I turned socialist at fifteen when we went bankrupt and I saw what the world was for most people."

"Noticed any improvement lately?"

"Worse. No steaks," my father muttered.

CARL AND I BEGAN CLEANING the kerosene lamps in Gavin's house in sullen silence. I didn't even ask for a story. Suddenly we heard geese honking overhead. Carl grabbed his gun and dashed outside but they'd passed over.

"Early migration, early winter," Dunham said.

"I could taste that roast goose," Carl said, coming back and stretching out on the bed. "I need a change."

I'd never tasted goose or steak either but they must be pretty good to put Carl in such a mood. He was never gloomy. I'd heard Doggett talking about mouth watering good steak, too. George Blais, a Dunite who was a vegetarian, said Doggett was a cold-blooded killer to even think about eating cows.

The next morning I woke to the blast of three shots and a thundering crash in the brush right outside our cabin, directly in front of where we were sleeping. Was this an earthquake?

Our dog, Dribbly, slinked to the door with his tail between his legs, whimpering.

"Oh, my God," Dunham said, pulling on his pants and rushing out the door. I was right behind him.

"Carl, what the hell? This isn't just a fine for clamming, you know. Besides, they're protected—what are you thinking of?"

Lying out on the sand and sage before us was the biggest bird I'd ever seen in my life, longer than my dad was tall and with wings that stretched as wide as our bedroom. Against the sand, sage, and lupine bushes the bird looked as big as a whale and tragically white.

Dribbly ran toward the huge bird, his teeth bared.

"No," Dunham yelled. "Dribbly, back, back! In the house." My father pushed my dog back in the house and slammed the door. I could hear Dribbly scratching on the door.

"What is it?" I asked, pointing to the bird.

"A swan," Carl said. "I must have been crazy to shoot. God, I'm sorry."

The swan's wings rose about a foot off the sand and flopped with a whoosh. The bird didn't move again. Wasn't there a fairy princess who got turned into a swan? There were tears in Carl's eyes and my father was madder than I'd ever seen him so I didn't ask about the princess.

"If the game warden heard those shots, we're in for it," Dunham was saying. "You could get San Quentin for killing a swan."

I started walking around the giant white bird. It seemed like a statue—or a miracle—so many white feathers, the neck alone almost as tall as I was. The swan's eyes closed as the sun rose over the dunes, bringing a sparkle to its feathers.

"The only thing I can say is I was so hungry," Carl whispered.

"Aside from everything else, there's no way in hell we can eat all this,

"A swan," Carl said. "I must have been crazy to shoot. God, I'm sorry." Carl Beckstead was a poet and photographer.
Courtesy of Lesley Gerber Benn.

even if we invite every Dunite for five miles around. Why didn't you wait for geese?"

"Next time I will," Carl said quietly.

My father and Carl stood there looking at the enormous bird for a while. Then they sighed and turned together and went inside. A few minutes later they came back out with coffee and cigarettes and stood staring at the dead swan again.

Dunham drank down his coffee and took a drag on his cigarette. "Well, I suppose it could have been worse. You could have hit two swans."

"We'd better bury those wings, feet, feathers, neck, and bones." Carl said.

Dunham nodded. "Start digging. I'm going to look for the leftover canning jars and seals I put away."

"I saved your cider jars too."

It took Carl and Doggett the rest of the morning to dig a hole big enough to dispose of what we couldn't eat, deep enough so the coyotes and Dribbly wouldn't dig it up. All the while we were terrified the game warden or the police would come walking down the willow path. Meanwhile Dunham was decapitating, skinning, and dumping the evidence. They worked all day. Carl plucked the swan while my father got ready to cook it, chunk by chunk, in the washtub. I had been gathering driftwood for the fire all afternoon, under strict orders not to talk to a single soul.

When it got dark they finally relaxed, figuring the danger from the game warden was about over. Carl carved enough steaks for all the nearby Dunites for two days, as long as he figured raw swan meat would last without refrigeration. Toward evening Dunham had filled the laundry tub with water and put the first big chunks of meat in to cook on the wood stove. Carl built a bonfire and roasted eight swan steaks but we were almost too tired to eat. I got a tummyache later. The meat had a strong gamey taste I wasn't used to. Carl ate three steaks and said he might be soul sick but his stomach felt better than it had in four years.

It took my father and Carl hours and hours to cook and can the swan meat that we weren't eating right away, as steaks, stew, swan burgers, and swanghetti. After the game warden didn't show up that first day both men seemed rather proud of themselves. They raked sand over bloody spots where they'd dragged the swan. Dunham told me Carl shouldn't have shot a swan but these were desperate times and there was a lot of meat to share if we kept cooking it up.

They took turns telling stories. Between stories we sang as we worked. Carl sang cowboy songs from growing up on a farm and a few sailor songs he'd picked up working on a fishing boat. Lonesome-happy songs, he called them. I sang the lullabies Marion used when she would sing me to sleep.

My father sang the songs he'd learned when he'd gotten picked up in Georgia for riding the rails, and spent six months in a chain gang. What happened was that his mother and stepfather went bankrupt in Paris from a shortfall at the early Metro Goldwyn Mayer Studios where his stepfather was a vice president. The sheriffs came to Long Island and took over the family home, the family photographs, and Dunham's chow dog late one night. Dunham was fifteen and staying home alone at the time. He was furious because the police had taken his dog so he and his friend, the son of the New York Stock Exchange president, hoboed down South.

"We'd never ridden the rails before, either of us. It wasn't hard but when we hopped off the freight car in Georgia, the local sheriff put us in irons and hauled us right smack off to the chain gang."

"Just like that?" Carl asked.

Dunham nodded. "The whole country was looking for us while we were splitting rocks for six months. Then we were released without any money to make a phone call and only just made it out of Georgia before dark, when the sheriff warned us he'd pick us up again."

"Only twelve years from chain gang to changing the world." Carl laughed softly.

I was thrilled that my own father had been a hobo. Except that of course Dunham hadn't been dirty or sad like hoboes I'd seen. He said it was okay to visit hobo camps with a grown-up but not by myself.

"But I visit the Dunites by myself."

"We're talking about strangers and the Dunites are friends. I mean it."

There were so few rules in my life that it wouldn't have occurred to me to disobey one.

The actual chain gang experience took a few more years for me to visualize. I loved the wailing songs, even though Carl said Dunham was atonal so I'd have to learn the tunes later. My favorite began:

"Lost one night on a wild horse range, beside a flickering fire.

A coyote came and sat by me and this is what the coyote said:

Don't you know that your dreams are vain?

Don't you know that your hopes are false?

Don't you know ere the night is out, I'll be howling o'er your grave?"

ONCE WE GOT OVER THE SHOCK of getting the dead swan safely buried and cooked, we had a wonderful week together. It was something of a letdown when the last of the swan meat was canned and sealed. Our magic interlude was drawing to a close—though I was glad to go back to eating clam chowder. We were proud to contribute two shelves of canned swan meat to Moy Mell for the winter.

I felt sad on the day Gavin would be bringing my mother and the others home. We'd had such a good time, "batching" it. I could see a gentle grief in Dunham's eyes too.

"We've had a good time canning, Gooch."

I nodded.

"You two look like a couple of mackerel, just hooked," Carl said.

"We're fish out of water sometimes. But this winter you'll have canned swan meat so don't complain."

"I wasn't." The three of us smiled at each other. Carl's usual good humor had been restored by canning swan.

When the others came walking down the willow path that evening, Dunham had swanghetti for all, ready and waiting.

That winter, when the last geese flew low over the dunes, honking mournfully, breaking formation and honking, circling again and again, "searching for a lost mate. It's enough to break your heart," my mother said, shading her eyes against the sun and staring up into the sky for a long time.

Carl shot two geese and Gavin and my father cooked a feast. That night rains hit Moy Mell so we ate inside, which meant everyone huddled close, listening to the rain on the roof, promising to take leftovers to Arther and Doggett tomorrow, or when the rain stopped.

Pretty Dolores sometimes said she was my morning mother and, in a way, she was. She'd comb my hair and read with me and sometimes we'd talk until Marion woke up. So I suppose she had some reason to ask that night if I would be going into town to live with Dr. Gerber's family and go to kindergarten, though this was the first I'd heard of it.

I saw Carl and my mother frown at her.

"Do I have to?"

"Would you like to go to school?" my father asked.

"No, you don't have to," Marion said.

I was quiet for a long moment. I wanted to learn to write. A lot. But leave Dunham and Marion, leave everyone in the dunes? Leave Dribbly? Leave Dancer just when Carl was teaching me to milk her, though my fingers weren't strong enough to do it alone yet. "Can't you teach me to write?" I asked my father.

It felt to me as if everyone in the room were holding their breath.

"Sure, I'll teach you to write. It's a deal," Dunham said softly.

Dolores went out on the back porch to have a cigarette. Marion and Carl had their heads together, whispering. I hated it when grown-ups had secrets from me. It would have been fun living with a real family who had three girls to play with like the Gerbers did—but I wasn't going anywhere.

Jack Reed, Marion's friend Jack, and Dolores, standing.
Seated: Dunham, Ed Sherron, Marion.
Courtesy of Dr. R. W. Gerber Family Papers.

A FEW WEEKS LATER Dr. Gerber made a house call to the dunes because the game warden told him that Aussie Slim's delirium tremens were worse. He brought his family along to Moy Mell for the day. The Gerbers' three daughters were about my age and I loved playing with them. Barbara was six, a year older than me. Lesley was six months younger and Catherine two years younger than I was.

Their parents and mine were all in their late twenties, and they'd even bought their wedding rings from the same jeweler in Los Angeles, but the Gerbers were homier together somehow. More kids. Big Cathie had long prematurely grey hair that she pulled back into a knot with fresh flowers behind one ear. She had a soft voice and a way of looking at you with her big grey eyes that held all the love in the world. I thought she was the most beautiful woman I'd ever seen and most of the Dunites agreed with me. We called her youngest daughter Little Cathie.

During the afternoon, I showed Barbara how to shimmy under the willows and play spy. She was worried about poison oak but I'd never gotten it so she took a chance. Besides, poison oak turned bright shiny red in the fall, easy to see and avoid. The first people we spied were Dolores and my father, sitting on the back steps of the community house, kissing. She was on his lap.

"Oh, boy," Barbara said.

"Shhhhh."

I'd never seen Dunham kiss anyone but my mother, Marion, before Dolores, but there was no law against it, was there? Gavin was always kissing people. We watched another few minutes. Barbara had this funny staring look as she watched Dunham and Dolores. I got scared I might throw up so I began scooting backwards. When we reached the path leading to Arther's cove and could stand up again, Barbara said, "Only sissies cry, crybaby."

I had no idea I'd been crying but my cheeks did feel wet. Barbara was already in first grade and I wanted her to like me so I wiped my nose and my tears on some toilet paper I carried for bathroom calls to the outhouse.

"I wasn't crying. I got something in my eye," I said.

"Wanta go back then?"

I shook my head, trying to think of something—anything—to divert her. "Let's hunt arrowheads. Gavin pays a nickel a head."

"Nah. Too hard."

"Maybe Carl will tell us a story."

"Naaah."

"We can watch Arther draw devils and dye his hair."

Barbara shrugged but took off at a run for Arther's cove.

I whistled for Dribbly and went after her. I'd been getting up my nerve to ask Arther about Dunham and Dolores but not in front of Barbara. No, sireee.

WE FOUND DR. RUDY with the Dunites—Arther, Doggett, and George Blais. He'd finished examining Aussie Slim out by the beach. Then he'd checked over these three and they were having a shot of George's moonshine whiskey in their coffee. Arther and Doggett were in their fifties. George was in his sixties but he was going to outlast anyone in the dunes, according to the doctor.

"How come you've got a better body than I have?" Rudy asked George.

It was true that Rudy was short and a little heavy, but he smiled a lot more than George.

"Well, Doc," George said. "I'm a nudist, a walker, and a sun worshipper. I only eat vegetables, and I'm chaste."

"You and Doggett and I are all celibate, damn it," Arther said. "Nothing to brag about."

"Most of the time," Doggett said quietly.

"But you drink a fair amount of alcohol, George."

"Pure, Doc. None of that Dago red wine your patients pay bills with."

My mother thought the Gerbers had turned vegetarian because of the Depression. Most of Rudy's patients didn't have the money to pay cash and brought vegetables and eggs from their gardens instead. Some brought homemade wine; some came with crates of strawberries. My mother said the doctor never turned anyone away because they couldn't pay and he never complained that he didn't have more money. Instead, he built his house with used lumber and Big Cathie bought their clothes from the Santa Barbara Goodwill. Rudy had a patient in Santa Barbara who gave him cello lessons once in a while in exchange for osteopathic massages and sometimes he took Big Cathie. Sounded like fun. They went to the Goodwill store and bought clothes and quilts.

"Good barley brew never hurt any man, Doc," George said.

"Daddy, what's chaste?

I stared at Barbara. Her father was laughing and she looked blotchy red and mad.

"Daddy, I asked you a question. What is chaste?"

"It means he's not married, Barbara."

The men laughed together, at a joke they weren't telling us.

I had wanted to ask if George going naked made us a nudist colony like Carl Angelo, the grocer, said. It was true that he often didn't wear any clothes but why should that make the grocer mad? The rest of us wore clothes. Sometimes, on a warm day, my mother, my father, and I lay spread eagled out on the sand after a swim without clothes. The sun felt wonderful on my body. George didn't see why anyone wore clothes unless they were cold. That made sense, didn't it?

"It means he's not married," he repeated. Barbara was definitely not convinced.

I watched as Rudy got up, washed his hands and flexed them. I knew he was getting ready to give me an osteopathic manipulation on my legs and my back. He always did when he came to Moy Mell. Sometimes my legs hurt a little but I could walk better afterwards. I knew that one day I'd be able to choose whether to be a dancer or a photographer because of his help. Arther cleaned off his big wooden table, spread out a thick quilt and I climbed up and sat with my knees dangling over the table, grinning.

"You sure like being the center of attention," Barbara snapped.

"Don't we all," Dr. Rudy said as he massaged both sides of each leg from my hip to my ankle. "Circulation," he said. "Getting the circulation moving will strengthen the muscles she's got left from the polio."

At the same time Arther was washing my feet. Hard. "You're tickling me," I said.

He let go of my feet and we looked at each other.

Rudy said, "Well. A bath—or a swim—might help. Okay, turn over on your stomach and we'll work on your back and upper legs. We'll let walking over the sand dunes take care of your feet."

SO MUCH WAS HAPPENING in Moy Mell that wet winter and spring. Gavin was away most of the time, trying to get money so he could continue publishing *Dune Forum*. Dunham later told me that they felt insight and original thought were going down the drain for the want of such a very few dollars.

Gavin kept sending guests to Moy Mell, whom he might or might not be around to welcome when they showed up.

Once he came home and told us to expect a visit from India's outstanding holy man, the Sri Meher Baba, who would be in California to break a seven-year silence at the Hollywood Bowl and was stopping overnight with us at Moy Mell. The Hindus believed he was an Avatar like Jesus Christ and Mohammed had been. The Sri Meher Baba traveled with a retinue that sounded to my mother like the court of King Arthur. Princess Norina Matchabelli of the perfume family and Mrs. Patterson, heiress to the *Chicago Tribune*, particularly interested Marion.

But, before the Baba could come, a house had to be built for him. No one could use the house until after the Sri Meher Baba had slept there because he couldn't stay if it had been profaned. The Princess Matchabelli and her friends paid more than enough to have the guesthouse built. Everyone felt lighthearted because surely *Dune Forum* couldn't be dying if this most famous and holy of Indians was having a house built just so he could stay overnight with us.

It was during the building of the Sri Meher Baba's guesthouse that I got to know Sammy Cohen, a Dunite who lived in a cove about a mile down the dunes, near the poet Hugo Seelig. Gavin and the heiress Mrs. Patterson hired Sammy to help build the Baba's house because he'd become a devout Hindu and, therefore, the Baba would feel Sammy's good karma. Sammy had even read the Baba's writings. I became Sammy's shadow. He was young and laughed a lot and would tell me incredible stories of his father's sausage factories in Brooklyn. Sammy loved his parents but he had to leave because he'd converted to Hinduism and could no longer eat even kosher sausages.

I noticed he still ate clams and stupidly kept getting arrested for clamming because he couldn't lie to the game warden, even after I told him the game warden didn't want to catch Dunites. Meanwhile, the Baba's house got a roof and two windows but stood empty waiting because the great man had decided to go to India.

MY FATHER WAS SPENDING more time away from the dunes helping Upton Sinclair organize his campaign for governor of California. My mother was spending more time in bed reading. Gone were the times with the three of us cuddled together in bed laughing and telling stories. Some weeks we didn't even go swimming together. I didn't blame Pretty Dolores for this. I was a little uneasy after watching her kiss my father but I still liked her. I blamed Upton Sinclair running for governor of California.

And then, I don't remember how or even when, I became aware of a tall dark good-looking man at meals. I heard Carl tell Mary he was an old boyfriend of Gavin's, who'd invited him up from Los Angeles. I noticed that the others would get this man off in a corner and tell him things. Sounded like their secrets. Was it because he was part American Indian or because he was a truck driver or because he just stood there listening, never taking his eyes off the person who was talking?

But even before Gavin left to raise money for *Dune Forum*, Jack seemed to be always at my mother's elbow. She would look up at him and her face would come alive. She'd light up with an expression she normally only had when she looked at me. Jack was willing to work in the vegetable garden.

The grown-ups liked him. But Marion looked at him with love that was meant for me and I was jealous.

One day Marion and I had just finished lunch when Jack walked into the room and headed toward her, smiling. I quickly climbed up on my mother's lap, locked my arms around her waist and lay my head on her shoulder. "Hey, Baby, what's this all of a sudden?"

I didn't say a word, just hung on and made the meanest face at Jack.

Jack frowned back. "Oh, shit," he said, then turned and walked out, slamming the door behind him.

"Jack," Marion called.

"I hate him," I said.

"Oh, you two," she murmured, giving me a kiss on the cheek. We sat there. In a few minutes I climbed off her lap. My mother got up and went after Jack.

CHAPTER

6

In the fall of 1934 I was six and had to start first grade. I had to leave
Moy Mell. We couldn't commute or put it off any longer. My father made
moving to town to live with the Gerbers an adventure. He and Gavin had
come home without enough money to put out another *Dune Forum* right
away but they had enough to buy me clothes, to "launch Ella in the big wide
world, the working world beyond the Depression," as Dunham put it.

"It's a proud moment for Marion and me. You're ready for school, a
giant step toward independence. And I know the Gerbers will take good
care of you."

"Ah, but she's still my baby. Aren't you, darling?" Marion sighed.

Oh, I hope she doesn't cry, I thought, knowing I was making some kind
of choice, not only living in Oceano so I could go to school but taking sides
with my father. I didn't know why or how exactly but I knew my mother's
smile with Jack figured in here somewhere.

Dunham collected our car Belinda from the Varians' Halcyon garage once again so we would only have to walk out from Moy Mell to the beach where the car was parked. Dunham carried a gunnysack of his clothes over one shoulder and a gunnysack of my clothes on the other shoulder and dumped them into the rumble seat. My mother held me tight but my father opened the car door and I eased into the front seat. We sped off in Belinda, up the beach at low tide to Oceano, to our new lives, leaving Marion shading her eyes with one hand, a lonely figure staring after us.

Dunham and Ken Schussman pulled a house trailer all over California that fall of 1934, speaking to workers on farms and in factories and at meetings of men and women who had lost their jobs, telling them that Upton Sinclair and the Democratic Party were the political future for the man and woman who wanted work. Arther had painted their slogan EPIC on one side of the trailer. End Poverty In California. My father wrote daily press releases and news articles. Turning the Democratic Party toward socialist ideals was exciting and he believed that Upton Sinclair and the people around him could pull California out of the Depression. He loved being part of what he saw as a new beginning. Whenever I saw my father that fall he looked happy.

BEFORE HE LEFT, HE BOUGHT me shoes, socks, underwear, a pleated plaid skirt, and a yellow rain slicker. They didn't have quite the aura of the clothes the Gerbers found in the Santa Barbara Goodwill but they were Dunham's gift and that made up for their being new. Besides, even the Gerber girls didn't have a great-grandmother in England who knit all their sweaters like I had. When great-grandmother Nannie lost her money she had herself declared England's champion knitter and went around the world on passenger liners giving lessons and visiting relatives on every continent while she knit Dunham and me sweaters.

My mother told me of trying to watch a movie while Nannie and Dunham, who was a grand master, got bored. They played chess in their heads across her. My father and Nannie didn't need a board or chessmen. They could figure the possible moves in their heads. In fact, those two could play two or three people at a time. My great-grandmother had also poured strong tea into nursing bottles to stimulate my thinking. Marion thought it was just as well that Nannie only made the journey to California every four years or so.

The Gerbers had a lovely house that Gavin called a bungalow. Rudy had built it himself, with the help of friends. Many of the materials had been contributed by others who had finished building their own places. One man might have leftover lumber and another some extra windows. Gavin gave Rudy a fireplace. Rudy was the best and wittiest doctor around so everyone did what they could to help him stay in Oceano.

The kitchen was the heart of their house, with a big wood stove and a mammoth table. It was separated from the living room by cabinets as high as my head so Big Cathie and Rudy wouldn't miss living room conversations when they were working. Vaulted Chinese-red ceilings gave the house a larger feeling. The front door opened into a patients' waiting room between the living room and the doctor's office. We could hear what the

Dr. Rudy Gerber, center, with Little Catherine on his knee and
Big Catherine to their right. Arther Allman stands beside Catherine,
smoking his pipe. Near left, standing, are Pete Koski and Doggett.
Courtesy of Dr. R. W. Gerber Family Papers.

patients said if we listened hard, which we did if there was a prostitute or someone we knew in the waiting room.

Cathie and Rudy's bedroom was behind the doctor's office. The bathroom, equipped with my first flush toilet, was across the hall in the middle of the house. I was proud of that toilet but I was afraid of all the swirling water too. Suppose the toilet sucked me down inside itself?

The day I moved in they were finishing the kitchen table, built from a ten foot oak slab with which a patient had paid his doctor's bill. Rudy had made a platform under the table. Barbara and I could almost touch the platform with our feet. He'd made boxes for Lesley and Little Cathie's feet because they were too small to sit tall at the table like Barbara and I did. He bolted the table to the platform floor and built one long U shaped bench attached to the walls so friends could squeeze in if they dropped by for dinner. There was a wall of windows behind the table so we could watch birds in the garden.

"Does it fit? Are you comfortable, Ella?" Rudy asked as if my fitting were the most important question in the world.

"Oh, yes. I love this table," I said and they all laughed.

"We want you to be happy with us, Ella. Don't we, kids?"

"Then we better show her where she's going to sleep," Lesley said.

We all trooped downstairs to the kids' room. Rudy had built three bunk beds with drawers underneath. The mattresses were new; the down quilts came from Santa Barbara's Goodwill store. I had a folding cot. We each had a closet and a big drawer. My doll, given to me by Marion Davies, and a dozen of my books went into my big drawer. Beyond the bunks was a wall with windows looking out into the garden.

"I have lights so I can read," Barbara said. "Of course, Lesley and Catherine don't know how yet."

"But I start kindergarten on Monday," Lesley reminded Barbara.

"Who cares?" Little Cathie asked. She'd be the only one who couldn't read and she'd be home alone. Cathie was three and would one day be a very talented painter.

That night Dunham and Carl were both with us for dinner, eight of us around the new table. Later, I showed them my home, saving the toilet until last. Carl nearly broke my bed trying it out. Then my father walked through the young garden eating plums and telling me the names of the vegetables Rudy had planted.

"And best of all, Dr. Rudy made the table especially so it would fit Barbara and me. He waited until I got here today to finish it."

"Lucky you," Dunham said and wiggled his ears. He didn't seem as excited as I thought he should be so I reached out and took his hand. We grinned at each other.

It was only late that night when the Gerber girls had gone to sleep and I could hear Rudy playing the cello upstairs that I wondered why my mother hadn't walked up from the dunes with Carl. She wasn't much of a walker but you'd think she'd want to see where I was going to live. She was different lately. She didn't play with me. She was either lying in bed staring at nothing or she was with Jack. Still, if I listened carefully here in Oceano, I could faintly hear the sound of the surf rolling in onto the beach just as I could at Moy Mell and that helped. My mother had told me she'd be hearing the waves breaking too and thinking of me. When I left she said if I listened I could feel her sending her love. I did feel her love. She'd come soon. I could go down to the dunes whenever there was a holiday and someone could walk with me. And my father had come today. He said he'd come often. Still, I went to sleep that night and many nights thinking of Marion and Dunham and me, cuddling in their bed at night, saying goodnight the way we used to.

MONDAY MORNING BARBARA AND I were up early eating our oatmeal with strawberries and cream. I could see that living with vegetarians wasn't going to be so hard.

But nothing prepared me for school. I'd seen those two fairytale wooden buildings with bell towers, set in a semicircle of eucalyptus trees, facing toward the beach from the Gerbers' house. One building housed kindergarten through third grade and the other held fourth through sixth graders. I was raring to go to school. I could read *Little Black Sambo* and *Billy*

Whiskers but I wanted to read Zane Grey's cowboy stories and the *Iliad* like Carl did. I wanted to write a letter to great-grandmother Nannie in England like my father did.

As we walked to school Barbara did mention that a few kids didn't always wear shoes but since we were the doctor's family we had to. I was so pleased to be included in that "we" that I hardly noticed her gloom. Then we walked through the playground. Never mind the shoes. I was the only kid I saw with any new clothes! I stood out like a sore thumb. The schoolyard was filled with cold kids in old clothes and tennis shoes with holes in them.

Miss Freeman, our teacher, introduced me as coming from Moy Mell but living with Dr. Gerber's family. The kids whispered and giggled. At recess they had a lot to say.

"Ella, you're the girl from the nudist colony, ain't you?"

"Don't play with her or you'll turn into a nudist too. Her duds are new because she didn't have clothes. They had to buy her something to wear."

"My old man says they don't believe in marriage down there. Free love. Free love. Free love. Tramps, all of them, Ma says."

"My parents are too married," I shouted.

Some kids would whisper, some would yell. Miss Freeman gave me a hug and told the class to stop teasing me, which made it worse. Even Barbara Gerber seemed ashamed to be seen with me.

I got so mad I could hardly remember the alphabet, let alone read the rhyme about Jack jumping over the candlestick. I'd been having trouble seeing the blackboard even before I got mad. The letters looked fuzzy and I'd have to walk up and try to memorize them during recess.

Then the teacher thought Lesley seemed bewildered when she showed up for afternoon kindergarten so Barbara got out early to take her little sister home. But I had to stay until the bell rang. Barbara said I should just keep walking up the road until I got to the Gerber house. It was the only house with orange and turquoise window frames. I'd see the Dr. Gerber sign hanging out in front.

I walked through the eucalyptus grove out to the road. Four girls in my class were waiting for me. They started chanting and the eucalyptus buds they threw at me stung.

"Let's take her clothes off so she'll look like the nudist she is."

"Go back where you come from. You don't belong with decent people."

"You're white trash!" I didn't remember hearing the term but it stuck. They were insulting the Dunites! "White trash! White trash!"

I kicked sand at them and then I hit the closest girl in the jaw. She ran away crying! I lit into the next girl and socked her in the stomach. She fell down. I'd never been in a fight but, hey, I wasn't a nudist either. And my parents were so married. The third and fourth girls came at me together. I tripped one and the other spit at me. I spit back and turned and ran toward home.

I heard footsteps behind me. I tried to run faster but my feet hurt from running. I was crying so hard I kept stumbling in the new shoes and my chest hurt so I could hardly breathe.

"Ella, wait for us! We just want to walk home with you."

"Yeah, to help you."

Boys? Boys chasing me? To help me? I doubted that but my side hurt and my legs hurt with that awful tired polio hurt Rudy said I should never let them get. I knew my legs would hurt all night and tears filled my eyes. I could hardly stand up. So I turned and faced them.

"I'm Billy Angelo. My dad owns the store. He likes you," a boy with curly black hair and gentle brown eyes said.

I nodded. His father said I came from a nudist colony but he gave me candy anyway.

"And I'm Harold Guiton. We'll walk you home any old time." Harold was taller, skinny with sandy colored hair and a kind look. I trusted him right off.

"Your dad's rich," I managed to say. Both boys were in my class. Harold and Billy and I smiled at each other. We were friends.

Harold and Billy walked me home to the Gerbers' that day. I'd like to say that stopped all the mean teasing but that's too easy. However, they were my first friends. Also, fighting those girls did make them hesitate to pick on me. Miss Freeman was loving and taught me to read and write and that helped a lot.

Big Cathie and Rudy were disappointed that I'd torn my blouse and gotten so dirty. I was ashamed to tell them the girls said I lived in a nudist colony. That night I hung my new clothes forever in the back of the closet and the next day I wore one of my old faded dune skirts.

It took me another week to get rid of the new leather oxfords. Finally, I started hiding my shoes behind a rock in a field and picking them up and putting them on again on the way home. This worked for a while but, after a month or so, I came to the field one afternoon to find it plowed under, my shoes along with the weeds and goldenrod. I'd turn over little pieces of brown leather shoes as I sifted through the dirt.

"He'll spank you," Barbara said tearfully.

Not me. I'm company, I thought.

But Rudy did spank me, explaining that shoes required cash, as much cash as the goat he'd been saving two months to buy, a goat that would have given milk and cheese.

"Kids beat me up if I wear those shoes," I sobbed.

"Don't talk back to—" but Rudy stopped in mid-sentence. He'd heard me. He knew the Oceano School parents had no jobs and could barely feed themselves on what the county gave. They were his patients, after all. He knew hungry kids could get mean.

"The kids who wear sneakers. They don't get beat up," Barbara said.

"*Gott im Himmel!*" Her father swore. Then he nodded. Just to be on the safe side, we bought our sneakers at the Goodwill.

A FEW DAYS LATER DUNHAM drove up in the EPIC trailer with Gavin. My father and I were playing checkers in the trailer and Gavin was reading an hour later when Upton Sinclair knocked on the door. Dunham said that, if I'd keep "the lip buttoned," I could stay while they talked about campaigning. It shouldn't take long. Gavin and Sinclair had to get to a meeting. I'd been missing Dunham and Marion and Moy Mell so I said okay though

I knew it would be hard to sit and listen to bossy Upton Sinclair go on and on. He ignored me as he came in.

"The *Los Angeles Times* and the *Chronicle* aren't running my articles," Dunham said, right off. "Editor takes the article, says he'll run it tomorrow and the damn thing never appears."

"Hearst and the movie studio heads have put the kibosh on it. They don't want voters to read my idea that people could have as much land as they can work themselves. Big business has most of the land now. Got any friends who can help us, Gavin?"

"Some. Myrna Loy and her husband could help in Hollywood. Helen Gahagan and Melvyn Douglas—"

"Good. I'll talk to the editor of the Santa Barbara paper," Sinclair added. "Dunham, can you do a piece on the plight of the Okies, the people who came from Oklahoma looking for work? I don't suppose most of them are registered to vote but all the same—I'd like to run it in the *Epic News*."

"Sure. Something like this? I've been writing one page handouts and getting them printed up," Dunham said, handing one to Sinclair.

A silence fell while Upton Sinclair read Dunham's handout. He'd better like it! He'd just better. After he finished reading, he considered for a long moment.

"Damn fine writing. Can you do one or two a week for the next month? We'll print up enough to paper California. And keep up the newspaper stories too. We've got 'em on the run, boys. I feel it in my bones."

He and Gavin left a few minutes later with copies of the handouts and the last newspaper release.

My father wiggled his ears, pulled out the checkerboard, and we went on with our game. He wanted to teach me chess but I'd seen him beat person after person in five moves flat so I stayed with checkers. At least I had a chance with checkers if I could get some kings.

CHAPTER

7

That fall Oceano had its worst measles epidemic in years. Rudy's waiting room was jammed with patients from eight in the morning until eight at night. Some days it seemed like the whole town had broken out in spots. Half the prostitutes down the road in Pismo Beach got measles and infected their Filipino clientele, who got particularly sick. They were Rudy's patients. By October Rudy decided this measles was too severe for a recovering polio case to risk and I'd better spend a couple of months in Moy Mell. My first grade teacher, Miss Freeman, would send lessons home with whatever Dunite walked to town to pick up the mail.

I was relieved. I hoped the epidemic lasted until Christmas. I would miss Barbara, Lesley, and Cathie, but not my battles with the girls in the eucalyptus grove. Bill Angelo and Harold Guiton wouldn't have to rescue me for a while. As it turned out, all three of the Gerber girls would get measles with high fevers. I was delighted to migrate back to Moy Mell. I missed my mother. I'd had enough of other kids. I preferred my grown-up Dunite friends to anyone I'd met at school except the teacher who taught me to read and write.

CARL AND ARTHER SHOWED UP at the Gerbers' a week or so after the decision was made that I should leave. I walked back to Moy Mell with them. I inhaled the bracing salty fish smell of the ocean as we slowly made our way down the beach. The sea was a calm grey-green and Arther said the surf was purring like a cat. Pelicans cruised low over the water, fishing. I found seventeen sand dollars! I was home.

"Dribbly's been so lonely she spends half the day pestering me," Arther said.

"Have you put her in your Atlantis book?"

"She doesn't fit. Your dog's entirely too good natured."

"We going clamming tomorrow, Kid?" Carl asked.

"Sure, but there's no one to make the clam chowder, with Dunham off campaigning."

"You'll be surprised."

The Dunites were still in their coves but Moy Mell sounded like it had emptied out since *Dune Forum* folded. Marion had written that Carl and Mary and herself were the only people who lived there full time. The regulars, she called them. Gavin and Dunham would come for a week or so, bringing guests. Since I'd gone to town, Edward Weston had been taking Carl out with him and Carl was becoming quite a photographer. Steinbeck had come through with some friends and read a chapter from his *Tortilla Flat*. John's best yet, Marion wrote. She wrote nothing of Jack, and Arther told me he'd gone. I'd have my mother to myself.

There was enough to eat. There were always clams and fish. Carl and Doggett let everyone take what they needed from their vegetable gardens, planted in lush willow tree compost. George Blais shared what my father called his 200-proof wheat mash liquor. Gavin's mother still sent a case of champagne every month. My mother said that as long as you could get cigarettes and a beer now and then and survive without new clothes and medicine or extra blankets, the dunes were one of the better places to sit out the Depression.

"IS THAT MARION?" I YELLED, wondering if I had made her appear by thinking of her. She was too far down the beach to be sure but the woman was tall and thin and stood with one hip out like my mother did and she was waving a long red shawl. Then I noticed a dog swimming back through the surf. She shook herself at my mother's feet and I knew. Dribbly and my mother.

"Looks like you dynamited Marion out of bed, Kid," Carl said.

I started to run.

"Easy does it," Carl called after me.

But I kept running until I tripped over a sea lion carcass that had washed in with the tide, landing spread eagle over the dried spiky back. By the time Marion reached me I smelled like the rotting sea lion and was sobbing.

She picked me up and crooned *"The Owl and the Pussycat,"* the very song I'd been missing most of all.

"Why didn't you ever visit me?"

"Oh, Lordie, first I didn't want you to catch my flu—and then I got the world's worst case of poison oak." My mother and I clung to each other.

"But I kept waiting for you."

"I thought you'd be so busy with school and the Gerbers that I could wait until I felt better. I'm so sorry." She brushed back my hair with her hand.

Carl and Arther caught up with us and we walked on together. The four p.m. wind was blowing up, blasting us with sand and the smell of sagebrush as we turned in and climbed over the sand and willow ridge toward Moy Mell.

"Mary's baked bread," I said, sniffing as I reached the willow ridge above Moy Mell and turned back for a last look at the ocean.

"She's baking bread for you." Carl smiled.

I ran down through the willows into our cove, an oasis of wild grasses, lupine bushes and, because this was October, goldenrod. The lush cove was surrounded by miles of Sahara sand dunes dotted with Indian shell mounds—sand as far as I could see and beyond. Moy Mell, I remembered, was Gaelic for the land of honey. A eucalyptus and cypress grove kept the live sand from covering our houses. How could people live in towns when they could live here? Dribbly trotted along by my side. Dancer, my goat, whose great dripping udders needed milking, came leaping through the sage and goldenrod. She rubbed against me. I leaned down and kissed her. She bleated. Dancer remembered me. I kissed her forehead

"I'd better milk her," Carl said with a sigh.

That night we ate perch grilled with corn over a bonfire and had Mary's bread for dessert. It was the first fish I'd had in a month because the Gerbers were vegetarians. Doggett, Arther, and George Blais came to dinner. The moon was almost full, and when coyotes howled we could look up and see my four friendly coyotes silhouetted at the crest of the dunes. They'd be shy of me again—for a while.

My mother played her violin for me. Then she stroked my hair and hugged me while Doggett and Arther played the fiddle and banjo. We all sang and told stories. I got the guest treatment, loving every minute, and I was grateful to the measles epidemic that made it all possible. Later, my mother and I lay in bed with our arms around each other and drifted off to sleep to the sound of the surf, the perfume of lupine and sage. I was home.

THE NEXT FEW DAYS I visited every Dunite. Each one had some horrible story of his own school days to tell me. Arther's teacher in Dublin rapped his arms and legs with a ruler that raised welts. Doggett's schoolmates ran his jacket up the flagpole and stole the pennies and nickels that fell out of his pockets.

I even hiked down to Hugo Seelig's cove. The other Dunites called Hugo *the* dune poet. They knew he'd had a nervous breakdown and come to the dunes to get his voice back, then stayed because he liked being a poet better than being a stockbroker. He had a rat named Beady Eyes who made his nest in Hugo's poetry. He looked up from the book he was reading as I slid down the last dune to his cove.

"Hi, Hugo. I'm back."

"I've been waiting for you, young lady. I have a present for you." Hugo rummaged in one of his knapsacks until he could hand me a bracelet filled with gold dust.

All the gold dust sparkled out of the bracelet in my hand. "So beautiful," I whispered.

"I won this in Las Vegas and have been on the lookout for my young lady with the golden touch."

I flushed as Hugo pushed the bracelet on my wrist. That bracelet represented femininity to me for many years and was my favorite possession in the world. I wore it when I got married.

LATE ONE AFTERNOON, AFTER I'D been back in the dunes about three weeks, Dunham and Gavin walked into the community house. Everyone except Aussie Slim and Irish Arther had hiked into town to vote for Upton Sinclair for governor of California the day before. Even Marion had walked in and voted. I'd stayed home with Arther since he couldn't vote. My father, born in Jamaica, was British so he couldn't vote either. We had no radios so we were eagerly waiting for someone to come and tell us who would be our new governor.

Carl and I were refilling and cleaning kerosene lamps when they walked in. I ran to Dunham and hugged him. He rubbed my head but didn't say a word. He had what my mother called his "the world's no damn good" look on his face. It was a little scary.

Carl looked at the exhausted, grim, unshaven faces. "Bad news?"

They both nodded.

"Clam chowder? Coffee?" Carl asked.

He handed chowder to Gavin and coffee to Dunham.

"Upton Sinclair lost?" Carl asked finally and then he gave me a little push. "Go call your mother and Mary."

"Merriam won."

We got back as my father pronounced Merriam governor of California. "What happened was this. Almost every farmer in the state sent out layoff notices to their workers, the layoffs only to take effect if Upton Sinclair were elected. The workers were afraid to vote. The employers' goons were at every polling place, writing down the names of anyone who voted."

"They kept legitimate voters away and then they stuffed the ballot boxes," Gavin added.

"What about Los Angeles?" my mother asked, taking my father's hand.

"Same damn thing. Factory workers and the unemployed were afraid to cross the thugs who hung around the polls," Gavin said.

"So we lost?" Carl rolled a cigarette and handed it to my father.

"Close but we lost," Gavin said with a sigh. "California lost her whole damn future by less than a hundred thousand votes."

My father lit his cigarette and took a long drag. We were all quiet and even the breakers hitting the beach seemed subdued.

"Did many of Roosevelt's people win?" There was hesitancy in Carl's voice.

"Yes, Franklin got most of the governors, thank God. At least that," Gavin said.

"That's important for the country," my mother said quietly. "So now what?"

"What do you think, Marion?" Dunham asked in a strange voice.

A silence fell over the room.

"This is no time for personal politics. We're all too tired," Gavin said finally.

What were personal politics? My stomach cramped and I tried to grab my mother and father's hands but they were too far apart so I settled for my father, standing next to me. I wished they'd stop staring at each other like they were strangers.

"Gavin and I were talking about taking that trip to New York, attending the Mankind United meeting. We'll try out some ideas I've had. You know, the Utopian ideas. I have to try to help." He spoke directly to Marion.

"Mankind untied," my mother murmured, looking down. "How long?"

"We have to try," Gavin said.

Dunham frowned. "Three or four months."

"You'll be at school while we're gone and we'll write each other," Dunham added gently as I pulled on his hand.

"But New York's way far away. Is Marion going too?"

"No, Baby, I'll be here."

"No, Gooch. She'll be here."

They spoke at once. As if this was something they'd already talked about. But when? How soon would I learn enough to write a letter to my father?

MY FATHER AND GAVIN STAYED in the dunes a week while they were making preparations for their trip. Dunham and Marion and I still slept in the little room at the back of the community house but it wasn't so cozy anymore. Sometimes at night I'd hear my mother mutter "God damn you," and my father would get up and pace around outside, smoking.

"This time apart might clarify things for us," Dunham said another night.

Dunham Thorp reflecting.
Courtesy of Lesley Gerber Benn.

The next day I asked Arther what clarify meant.

"What did Marion say?" he asked.

"She said, "Ah, Dunham, if our life together were only that easy.""

"Then I don't think clarify means a damn thing."

"Why?"

"Don't worry so much. I hear your father's making 50-proof apple cider over there." Arther grinned. His red-brown, grey, yellow, and blue striped hair fell over his face and his blue eyes were kind. "Think he could use some help?"

So I ran back to core apples. Dunham and I spent those days laying in food for my mother and those of us staying in Moy Mell. Several gallons of hard cider with a kick to it took the place of wine. He also canned spaghetti sauce and tomatoes, boiling the bottles in the washtub, telling me stories of his family as he worked.

"My family was British and we have cousins and uncles on five continents. My grandmother didn't only demonstrate knitting on ships. She sailed from continent to continent keeping the family together. Nannie's only brother had a coffee plantation next to her in Jamaica but they haven't spoken in more than twenty-five years. If my grandmother happened to be in Jamaica no one could even invite them to the same party," he said, laughing.

I'd never heard Dunham talk much about his family before and it was unsettling. Marion had said he was a little ashamed because they were people who exploited workers, but he sounded proud, especially when he said he might inherit a barony some day. Why was he telling me now when he was going away to New York? Wasn't he coming back?

"When are you coming back?" I asked.

"A few months. Depends. I'll keep you posted."

"But you are coming back?"

"I'll always be back for you."

"Always?"

"All our lives."

Dunham, Gavin and Jack Reed standing before Belinda,
our car, on their way to Mankind United in New York.
Courtesy of Dr. R. W. Gerber Family Papers.

THAT WEEK I SELDOM LEFT my father's side. We worked on the canning and played checkers together from dawn to bedtime, except when I was doing my lessons for school. Still, his stories worried me, as if they were priming me to remember strangers. Why did I need to know where they lived? Unless he was leaving me.

Marion sometimes told family stories late at night but they were Irish Catholic stories. Her grandfather played violin in New York bars and went to work in a snowstorm one night against her grandmother's wishes. He died of pneumonia a week later. His wife, left with eight kids, never forgave him for dying. Nor did his youngest daughter, Marion's mother, who had planned to be an opera singer and instead married a house painter. She never forgave her husband or her five children either. "Oh, Lordie, Mama even padlocked the refrigerator," my mother would end that story, forgetting that I'd never seen a refrigerator.

All week Marion lay in bed smoking, reading magazines, and muttering, "Isn't our life hard enough without you going off again, Dunham?" *Saturday Evening Post, Liberty, Life,* Westerns, and *Colliers* lay across her bed like a patchwork quilt. She'd come in for meals and she and Dunham were friendly. It was only when I'd wake up at night that I'd hear their hushed angry whispers, my father pacing the room, the smell of their cigarette smoke. I lay very still in bed then, pretending to sleep. And the next morning I turned those memories off.

"AH, DUNHAM," MY MOTHER SAID on the day my father and Gavin left for New York, "even the skies are crying because you're leaving us." She was right. It started raining as they got into the old Dodge they'd be driving across country.

The day the skies cleared again Jack hiked over the dunes into Moy Mell. He'd come back from Los Angeles to see my mother again. I wondered if the measles epidemic was over.

8

Though I had hoped he was out of our lives and in Los Angeles, there was no mistaking Jack for anyone else. He was the tallest man I knew, and powerful. He had the high cheekbones and piercing brown eyes of his California Indian forefathers, stern and handsome. He was sure of himself and walked like a chief. I wondered if the Indians who'd lived in the dunes thought they were chiefs, as Jack seemed to.

"Gavin's not here, Jack," Carl said.

He shrugged and walked across the community house living room, took my mother in his arms and kissed her, as if he had every right in the world. I watched my mother's face light up, saw her kiss Jack and the measles epidemic in Oceano was over for me in that moment. It was time to go back to the Gerbers'. I began talking about missing Barbara, Lesley, and Little Cathie.

"Marion, do you know how far behind I am in arithmetic and reading?

I keep telling you!" Actually, I'd never thought of being behind, let alone mentioned arithmetic before.

Jack helped. "What goes on here? You're keeping this girl out of school because of an outbreak of measles for God's sakes? Who does Rudy think he is? She won't pass first grade!"

Jack wanted me out of his way in Moy Mell. I wanted out. We hurt my mother but it was Jack's fault and he didn't care.

"Ah, you two." She sighed and she and Jack exchanged a look so tender it made me want to kill them both.

Jack stood there, giving me the evil eye, his arm still around my mother's waist.

CARL SET OFF FOR TOWN the following week. It was a cold showery day in the first week of October. He brought back mail and supplies and the news that all three Gerber girls were over their measles. Rudy thought it was safe enough for me to return.

"MY BABY, YOU'RE LEAVING ME again," Marion moaned as I started packing my gunnysack.

"I'm supposed to go to school." Even school would be better than watching Jack and my mother looking at each other as if there was no one else in the whole world.

"Let's wait until it stops raining so we won't get pneumonia," Carl said quietly.

That night I was lying in bed with my mother's arms around my shoulders. She told me how much she would miss me. I felt like crying but I didn't want her to tell me again that I'd like Jack when I got to know him. We'd been through that that afternoon. Missing me served her right. Her voice was just above a whisper when she murmured that she'd had little tenderness in her life and Jack had this wonderful tender streak.

"You don't understand this yet but one day you will, darling."

I burrowed my head under her chin. I remembered hearing her use the word tender late at night with my father. I liked the word. Maybe Dunham didn't? I remembered Dunham holding Pretty Dolores on his lap and kissing her and had to admit the difference was I liked Dolores and didn't like Jack. She could be part of our family but not Jack. Never. Still, I kept wondering about grown-ups being tender and pressed close to Marion as we drifted asleep.

The next morning was cloudy but dry so Carl and Arther decided to take me to town. Jack was up, drinking a bottle of my father's 50-proof apple cider, alone in the community house dining room. I had seen him throw dishes and chairs when he drank so I was anxious to get going. We stared at each other.

"See you another day, Kid."

"I live here."

"Then stop sneaking around, for Christ's sake."

Gavin said I was a sneak, too. Suddenly, I stuck my tongue out at Jack. I'd never done that before, to anyone. I smiled, scared.

Jack sprung up, furious.

"You just leave me alone or I'll tell," I cried.

Jack stared at me, his fists working at his sides. I was plenty scared but it was hard to resist sticking my tongue out again. Finally, he sat down.

"You're a lousy spoiled kid but you're leaving, thank God." He took another drink.

I woke Marion with a cup of coffee and asked her to visit me at the Gerbers'. She said she might move to town in the spring if she could find a job.

"Without Jack?"

"Ah, you two."

Marion and I clung to each other. Finally, I broke away and ran down the stairs, without going back through the community room where Jack was drinking my father's hard cider.

Carl, Arther, and I trudged along the willow ridge out to the ocean. Wind cut us to the bone. We hadn't gotten half a mile down the beach before Arther had to stop and rest. It was then that I noticed he was dressed in clean corduroy pants, a good looking red shirt and a heavy sweater, what he called the dune equivalent of black tie and tails.

"How come you're so snazzy?" I asked.

"Rudy wants me to get an x-ray in San Luis Obispo," Arther replied, letting sand run through his fingers.

"Like when we can see the bones in our feet in the shoe store?"

"Yeah."

"Oh." I'd never heard of people "getting" x-rays.

When we stood up to walk, Carl took Arther's gunnysack, containing an Indonesian head he was carving out of wood for Rudy, extra clothes, and Arther's *Lost Continent of Atlantis* manuscript, a pretty heavy load. Carl had a gunnysack of my clothes on his other shoulder.

For a while we were quiet as we trudged along. Then Carl asked me why I didn't make a little effort to get along with Jack.

"He looks at me with mean eyes, like those first grade girls who hit me."

Carl looked at me and rolled a cigarette

"He does have a bullying streak when he's drinking," Arther said. "But he's okay sober."

"Jealous, Ella?" Carl asked

"We'll never get to school, Carl. Hurry up." I started pulling Carl and Arther, who were walking slowly on wet sand left by the high tide. I didn't want Carl asking any more questions.

Carl ruffled my hair.

We trudged on. As we were climbing up the ramp from the beach, disturbing hundreds of screeching gulls, we saw Krishnamurti talking to Mr. Bernuti in front of the bait store. Krishnamurti was a holy man from India who my mother called the handsomest man in the world. Rudy said he'd once been a Theosophist here and came back to visit friends in Halcyon. He also dropped by the Gerbers' sometimes for a vegetarian dinner. Mr. Bernuti must have been the oldest man in Oceano, with a white beard that came to his waist. He lived across the street from the Gerbers and hung a bunch of bananas outside of his cabin. The Gerber girls and I were welcome to pick one, as long as we asked first.

Arther was tired again and squatted next to Krishnamurti. He lit his pipe. "Ah, I'll rest and absorb your good karma," he said.

Krishnamurti smiled and put his arm around Arther's shoulder.

Carl took me on to school. All afternoon I only half listened, getting ready to fight my way out of the eucalyptus grove after last bell. Barbara Gerber stuck with me. Bill and Harold met us at the grove. Our voices dropped to whispers as we walked under the trees and came out on the street but there were no kids waiting to beat me up. Not a one. Not that day nor ever again. What had happened? Hadn't I just come back from the nudist colony?

"Maybe it was Miss Freeman telling the class about your polio," Bill Angelo said.

"Maybe it was the measles. Anyhow, let's go! I'm freezing," Barbara said.

We waved goodbye to the boys and walked home. I didn't care why the kids weren't fighting me so long as they weren't. At their worst, the kids were better than putting up with Jack in the dunes. Like Carl said, you win some and you lose some.

We walked quickly. I was eager to get to the Gerbers' house, to see Lesley and Cathie, Big Cathie and Rudy. This was my other home, wasn't it?

But no one was in the kitchen. Big Cathie had left a note on the table saying she was napping with the little girls but would we please wake her.

Barbara went in to wake her mother and sisters and I stayed in the kitchen. I ran my hand gently over the table I loved. The wood stove still had coals and the room was warm. The kitchen smelled of freshly cooked chili beans. There was a vase with a rose on the table. Frieda the striped cat slept in the sun on a window ledge. I was seeing the Gerber kitchen and living room for the first time without people. As if the rooms were waiting.

Then Big Cathie opened the sliding door from the hall, followed by the three girls, all laughing and talking at once. When she saw me Big Cathie smiled and her kind grey eyes lit up. She was glad to see me!

"Carl dropped off your clothes. He's down at the post office waiting for the afternoon mail, and then he'll be heading back to Moy Mell." She put an arm briefly around my shoulder.

"Did you bring us anything, Ella?" Little Cathie, who was four, asked.

I brought out three sand dollars and handed them around.

We heard Rudy's car in the alley, then his quick sure steps coming up the walk.

"Here's our girl," he cried out, giving me a big hug. I was home again.

CHAPTER

9

I went back to Moy Mell as soon as school was out for the three week Christmas holiday. Rudy drove me down at low tide on a clear cold day. Half a dozen seals played beyond the breakers. The beach was covered with seaweed. It smelled fresh and salty. The minute Rudy stopped the car I jumped out and started turning cartwheels. I was home.

A WEEK LATER RUDY came down again with the news that he'd gotten a phone call from Princess Matchabelli of the perfume family, the princess who had paid to build the Sri Meher Baba's guesthouse in Moy Mell. Rudy didn't catch everything that she said because half the people on his ten-party line were listening in, rustling and coughing. However, he gathered that the Sri Meher Baba and his retinue of eighteen would finally be arriving in Moy Mell a day or so after Christmas.

Gavin had gone to New York to see a new girlfriend and no one knew where he could be reached. Gavin had, however, left money for sheets, blankets, pillows, and food, in case the Sri Meher Baba and his friends ever came. Marion was to help buy sheets. Rudy later claimed that he and my mother bought every sheet, blanket, and pillow for sale in San Luis Obispo. Then he borrowed flashlights and kerosene lamps from neighbors.

Everyone in Moy Mell worked getting the beds set up and the houses clean. But what should we do about food? Were all Hindus vegetarians? Did they eat anything but curry? Did we have to keep food from being profaned for the Baba as we had the house Sammy had built for the holy man? Did he need his own outhouse? Gavin and Dunham were our best cooks and they were away. In the end so many Dunites came by with clams that Carl dug potatoes, carrots, and parsley from his garden, milked Dancer, and he and Doggett made a washtub of chowder. Someone would eat it.

Then, using Rudy's car, Carl and Hugo Seelig collected gunnysacks full of vegetable culls from the packing shed. We piled them in the back seat of the car. Sammy and Rudy bought everything else, including a fifty pound sack of rice, on credit from Angelo's store. Carl Angelo figured that if a princess were involved, her credit must be good. He turned out to be right.

With all the food, there wasn't room in the car for Hugo and me so we walked back to Moy Mell.

Later we found out that the Sri Meher Baba and his disciples stopped to visit with the Gerbers on Christmas Day. Rudy was thrilled to have one of the most revered religious leaders in the world as his guest.

Hugo and I were nearing the path into Moy Mell when three touring cars filled with the Baba and his disciples passed us and slowed to a stop.

"Come on, Hugo. Let's hurry and catch up," I yelled.

But Hugo caught my hand and pulled me back behind a dune as Sammy Cohen greeted people tumbling out of the cars.

"Quiet, Ella. You can often learn a great deal by quietly watching and not barging in where we may not be wanted yet."

I pouted but Hugo was usually right so I crouched behind our dune and watched as men in flowing white robes helped the women and men in pants and windbreakers out of the cars.

"I thought the women would have long dresses and fur coats," I grumbled.

Hugo grinned but continued watching intently as the newcomers, led by a man with curly brown hair to his shoulders, pressed their hands together. It looked like praying, though no one said a word.

"That's the Sri Meher Baba," Hugo whispered.

We watched as they put on backpacks and started up the path by the willows. I thought they looked like a royal procession, everyone walking straight and proud.

By the time we got there, the Sri Meher Baba and his friends had walked around Moy Mell and the Baba had decided to stay in Gavin's house rather than the guesthouse that had been built and kept pure for him. He'd met Gavin in Hollywood and liked his vibrations. His aura. Princess Matchabelli and the heiress Mrs. Patterson could use the guesthouse.

Nothing this exciting had ever happened in the dunes. Here was a major Indian religious leader (an Avatar, Hugo said) coming to visit us before he broke his seven-year silence in the Hollywood Bowl. Our cove, Moy Mell, shone for the Baba. The dandelions were still out and the morning glories were starting to bloom. Eucalyptus and sagebrush flowers sweetened the air.

Every Dunite from miles around appeared, bearing gifts of food or drink, sitting quietly in a semicircle outside on a sand dune. Sammy and Hugo were invited inside the community house for an audience but I sat on a dune with Doggett. My mother was inside with the holy man and I grew lonely for her. I needed her arms around me. I longed for a song. I needed her to explain what was going on.

As if she'd heard my yearning, Marion appeared at the community house door, peering out, shading her eyes with her hand. Then she saw me and called, beckoning me to come.

"Get a move on, Ella. The holy man wants to meet you," Doggett said, helping me up.

I took off running.

A major Indian religious leader came to visit us.
Sam Cohen, Sri Meher Baba, Hugo Seelig and John Doggett.
Photo courtesy: Beloved Archives and Naosherwan Anzar.

"The Baba felt a child's karma and wants to meet you." Marion's face was glowing.

Inside the community house, tables had been shoved against the walls and the Baba's disciples and Moy Mell people sat at them or squatted in yoga position on the floor. The room smelled of incense. At one end of the room, on a low platform, sat the most beautiful man I'd ever seen. He had long curly brown hair and a big mustache and he wore a long soft white robe. His face was radiant. I hadn't seen the radiance from behind the dune. He nodded, with one arm stretched toward me. I froze.

Marion gave me a little shove. Then, as if I'd been hypnotized, I walked around people toward the Sri Meher Baba. I was six and a half. As I write, I can still feel the warmth of those brown eyes and his smile going straight to my heart.

He put his hand on my head and I felt warm all the way down to my toes. He pressed gently and I smiled. I knew he didn't speak. I remember a greenish slate and chalk but I didn't see him use it. He held an alphabet square in one hand. He had an interpreter. I meant to tell the Baba how much Sammy admired him but there was Sammy sitting next to him. I don't remember if I said a word but I do remember feeling blessed in the warm glowing light from his face. And I remember the happiness in my mother's eyes.

But the next thing I really registered was sitting back out on the dunes around a bonfire, eating clam chowder on a dark night with a new moon in the sky. There were more people that night than I ever remember seeing in Moy Mell at one time. The Baba had gone to bed but the rest of us were singing on the dunes late into the evening. It was a happy night. As my mother put it, we all felt blessed.

Early the next morning the game warden arrested Sammy Cohen for clamming without a license. Again. The Baba was only staying that one day so we were all worried that Sammy would not see him again. There was a big fine or a five-day mandatory jail sentence for illegal clamming.

However, Princess Matchabelli and Elizabeth Patterson, the *Chicago Tribune* heiress, bailed him out and late that day when the Sri Meher Baba left the dunes, Sammy went with him.

Rudy said that the Sri Meher Baba had consulted him medically and indicated his voice was rusty from disuse. He had already decided the world wasn't ready for him to break his silence yet and had cancelled the Hollywood Bowl appearance. But it bothered him that his voice wasn't ready either. Rudy gave him some voice exercises. As it turned out, the Baba maintained his silence the rest of his life.

The Sri Meher Baba and his disciples caravanned back to Los Angeles, taking Sammy with them. A week later Sammy returned to the dunes. Soon he left again after waking Rudy one night and asking to see where on the world globe the Baba lived. He was going there—that night. Sammy sent me a postcard with a picture of the luxury liner he sailed on, first class. I never saw him again. No one I knew heard from him until thirty-five years later when Rudy Gerber got a letter from Sammy. The return address was the Baba's ashram in India. Sammy's father had died and he was coming home to Brooklyn to run the family's kosher sausage factory.

I CAN STILL LOOK OUT and imagine the Baba and the Princess Matchabelli and the heiress Elizabeth Patterson walking over the tops of the dunes. I can close my eyes and call up the Baba, his robes blowing in the wind, with the women in jackets and jeans and berets on either side of him. The women were talking and it didn't seem to bother either of them that the Baba didn't say a word. I can still hear the waves crashing onto the beach behind them.

We were all quiet and gentle with each other for a while after the Sri Meher Baba and his friends left. There was a lot of meditating and talk of the soul.

"We're a bit hung over on spirituality," as Carl put it.

"He's the holiest man we'll ever meet," Hugo said and my mother noticed tears in his eyes.

I went back to the Gerbers' and finished first grade. In the dunes they ate curries for months, as long as the ingredients held out. Meanwhile, though I didn't realize it at the time, other food was running out.

Gavin's inheritances from President Arthur and his father had run out too. His uncle was still alive so no other inheritance had come through yet. There was no more money. The Moy Mell people were young and out of work and it was 1935. Gavin blamed bad karma from one of his previous lives for his inability to scrape together the few dollars *Dune Forum* would require. But I also heard him say, and it fascinated me, that the American Indians who used to live in the dunes found everything they needed to live growing wild. Gavin admired the Chumash Indians because they didn't need money.

"Money couldn't buy their lives," he said.

"Maybe not, but don't tell Doggett since his Social Security kicked in."

Even I knew Carl was talking about the fact that the Social Security Act had passed and Doggett became the first Dunite to get a pension. Other older Dunites walked into Oceano and applied, even though they weren't quite sixty-five. They claimed to be born in towns whose records were destroyed by fire. A few of them would eventually get pensions. But the Moy Mell people were young and wanted jobs. The whole country wanted jobs. Fortunately my father had work and earned enough money for my mother and for me to pay the Gerbers $25 a month to board me in Oceano.

I took four letters from Pretty Dolores to forward to my father. She'd written me that she had evening primroses growing in the flower box on her balcony just as Arther Allman said old Dunites sometimes did. She said she was homesick for me. Who was she homesick for if she sent Dunham four letters and me one postcard?

10

The summer of 1935 I started walking to the Halcyon library so Winonah Varian could read my father's letters to me. He wrote me twice a
week but none of us at the Gerbers' could decipher his handwriting, which
looked like a choppy sea. Only my mother, in San Luis Obispo awaiting the
birth of our secret, or Winonah in Halcyon could read his writing. I had
this terrible need to be sure my father was alive, to feel his arms around
me. So far, I had to make do with his letters from New York.

Dunham wrote he'd be coming home to California soon and I was
desperate to know when. He'd been gone many months. Would he be
here by July 14th for my birthday? Would he be here in time to make the
strawberry shortcake he made every year?

Instead, Dunham wrote back about Gavin's recent marriage. He wrote
of their success with Mankind United and the Utopian Society. The only
reason he'd made this trip was that he knew those groups could help lift

us out of the Depression. Winonah said that he wrote to me as if I were an adult. Okay, but what about coming home? Summer in New York was blazing hot. He couldn't wait to get back to me and the fog, she read.

I'd gotten into the habit of stopping by to visit people along the way to Halcyon. I was picking friends in Halcyon much as I had among the Dunites when I was in Moy Mell, except that now I usually visited women. They lived in little houses crowded with family photos. They grew flowers instead of vegetables. Ella Young showed me how to pray for animals in her cat graveyard. A German woman fleeing Hitler offered me iced tea and the chocolates her sister sent from Germany. Another lady asked me to help hide her Persian rugs because the tax inspector was coming and she feared he'd take her off Relief rolls if he found valuable rugs. Best of all, at the library I was allowed to borrow the most exciting children's books in the world while Winonah wrote out Dunham's letter and gave me a piece of fruit to eat on the way home.

"Remind that father of yours we all miss him."

I was more comfortable talking books and gardens with Halcyon ladies than trying to play with children, something I was having trouble learning to do, only partly because I didn't run as well as kids who hadn't had polio. Besides, everyone in Halcyon was a Theosophist. Winonah said this meant they shared both love and food, which was better than socialism where you only shared food. My mother said Theosophy was a mixture of the teachings of Jesus and of Hindu Avatars.

> *Dear Ella,*
>
> *Gavin and I are coming home to you, just as soon as we get a few bucks together. I won't be long now but this car isn't reliable and there are 3,000 miles between you and me. Strawberry short-cake day is coming but it may have to be a little late this year. I've landed a job cooking for a lumber camp in Northern California if I can make it up there by August.*
>
> *Love, Dunham*

Dear Dunham,

...You told me birthdays are sacred and I will be seven on July 14th. You've always made me strawberry shortcake on my birthday. I'll see you then.

Love, Ella Mary

THERE WAS ALSO MY MOTHER'S secret, which was getting hard to keep. For one thing my mother's stomach kept getting bigger and nobody in town seemed to think she was fat.

"Your mom sure looks pregnant," Barbara Gerber said, after Marion had come up to visit me on her way to live in San Luis Obispo.

"She does?"

"Are you so stupid you can't even tell?"

So what could I say? Of course I could see she was pregnant and Marion had even helped me feel the baby move and hear its heart beat. I wanted to ask Barbara if she was glad when Lesley and Cathie were born. But if I told anyone before my dad found out that meant I couldn't keep a secret. I was a Dune Gazette. I was a little spy. Barbara's eyes narrowed the way they did when she thought someone was lying. Barbara hated liars.

"Well?"

"How would I know?" I turned and ran.

AT LAST, WHEN I'D ALMOST given up hope, Dunham and Gavin pulled up in front of the Gerbers' front door late on the afternoon before my birthday. I was starting out for the library and almost missed them because they were in a strange Dodge.

"Hey, Gooch," Dunham called. "Want to help me carry in these strawberries?"

"Dunham!" I threw myself into his arms. He was alive! He was home.

After dinner that night Big Cathie asked him if he'd seen Marion yet, saving me the trouble and the possibility of spilling the beans. Big Cathie and I were hulling strawberries. Dunham was beating batter for his biscuit shortcake. He stopped and sat down at the table with us, spreading his hands wide.

"Yes, we pulled into San Luis last night. I think Marion and I understand each other pretty well now. I only wish Jack were more reliable."

"Rudy told him he needs to stop drinking."

"That would be a good first step." Dunham turned to me. "Marion will be here for your birthday party, Gooch. Gavin will bring Carl and Hugo up from the dunes and then go on to San Luis for her."

I wanted to ask if Jack was coming too but, somehow, I couldn't. And what did it mean that Dunham and Marion understood each other? Did he know about my little brother or sister arriving or didn't he? Was he happy about it? I'd like to ask him so I could figure out whether I was. My mother wanted to tell him. Keep your mouth shut, Ella, I thought.

"Did you see Pretty Dolores in New York?" I asked as we went back out to the car.

"Yes and she sent you a birthday present." My father handed me the gift, which turned out to be a red knit cap with silver hearts around the brim, the prettiest hat I'd ever had. "And wait until you see what your great-grandmother Nannie sent you."

"Oh, the hat feels so soft. What did Nannie send?"

My father grinned his lopsided grin and unlocked the car. "Nannie would feel there's no reason you shouldn't have this today," he said handing me a soft heavy package tied with a big golden ribbon. I ran inside and plopped it on the Gerber table.

"For my birthday."

"A blanket," Barbara said.

"Who's it from?" Lesley asked.

I tore open the wrappings. Inside was a many-colored hand-knitted wool afghan, every square different. It was big enough to cover my whole bed, so warm I'd never be cold again. "Oooooh, all the colors of the rainbow," I breathed.

"You'll never be cold again," Lesley said with a deep sigh.

"Nannie would appreciate a thank-you note," Dunham added.

THE NEXT DAY WE CELEBRATED. It's the afternoon I still remember when I think of birthdays. I loved all of us sitting around the Gerber table eating strawberry shortcake. Gavin brought ice cream, which we never had because the Gerbers had no refrigerator. Barbara, Lesley, Cathie, and I shared tissue-wrapped party favors from the Chinese store instead of presents and we each chose one an hour. I wore the gold dust bracelet Hugo had given me. All the grown-ups were drinking wine and laughing. Dunham and Marion looked happy together. Dunham and Gavin were telling their New York adventures. Everyone wanted to know when his friend Esther was coming to Oceano and if she and Gavin were married yet.

"Wait and see," Gavin said.

No one mentioned Jack. Rudy kept putting records on the windup phonograph. At dusk he lit us kids each a sparkler. Then he climbed up the water tower in the back yard and shot off Roman candles.

I heard Big Cathie whisper that she had some baby clothes left over from Cathie. She was saving them for Marion. So the secret must be out. Dunham must have noticed if Big Cathie and Barbara had. I'd ask Marion when I could get her alone; ask her that and some other things too. For one thing, I didn't remember ever seeing a baby close up. How did they go to the bathroom and could they chew food?

AFTER THE PARTY, MY MOTHER and father and I walked across the back alley from the Gerbers' to an empty house Hugo Seelig had built and lived in briefly before he went to the dunes. Then the Gerbers lived there before they built their house. We'd be spending the night there. We carried blankets and a roll of toilet paper for the outhouse.

Marion boiled some hobo coffee and Dunham built a fire in the fireplace. "I like that picture of a lupine and poppy field on the wall," I said sleepily.

"Hugo left it for me so I could have lupines and poppies all year long," Marion said. "Dunham, why don't you begin," she added, handing him coffee.

He was silent for a while. I peeled my orange. Marion twisted her hair and looked around. Looking for something to read, I thought. She had that sad look in her eyes. I heard owls hooting in the eucalyptus trees. Something was wrong.

"Your mother and I love you so much."

There were tears in Dunham's eyes and he looked over at Marion. My dad never cried. Those tears scared me.

"You've been what made all these years of sadness worthwhile," my mother said, relieving Dunham. "But we found that—life—is easier for both of us when we're apart."

"You'll go on living with the Gerbers for a while, Gooch."

I looked up at my father, a little sick. "Where will you be?"

"I'll be cooking for a logging camp in Mendocino until I can get on the WPA and then we'll see."

Marion put her arm around me. I gave each of them a piece of my orange. "Where will you be?" I asked her.

"Right here in this house. Hugo is letting me live here. We'll see you every day."

"You and Jack?"

We were quiet for a while after I brought Jack up, like I'd called in a ghost. I wasn't surprised at what they said, exactly, so why did I feel like crying? The Gerbers and the Soblers were the only people we knew who stayed married and together. Maybe Marion wouldn't be sad anymore. Gavin had gotten married again and he had a smile on his face. It must be natural. But when would I see my father? The three of us wouldn't be together anymore. I knew that much. I felt like throwing up. Would I have to see Jack and the baby in the bed with Marion like the three of us used to be? I couldn't!

But they were talking to each other and didn't like me to interrupt so I didn't ask. Dunham was saying something about filing for divorce when he could get some money ahead. Marion sighed deeply and said it wasn't Jack and her but the baby and her. "I told you yesterday, I don't think I can marry an alcoholic, Dunham. It's your family pride."

"I'm giving the baby my name."

"And we're grateful."

They were talking gently and I was only half listening, sleepy again, when I woke up at her mention of the baby.

"What about my brother or sister who's arriving? Is that still a secret?"

"Half brother or half sister," my father said, snuffing out his cigarette fiercely.

"Like Gavin and Loring?" That would be okay. My father looked down at the floor.

"God knows, it's no secret, anymore." Marion gave a little groan, lighting a cigarette. "She's falling asleep, Dunham. Could you set up her cot?"

The last thing I remember is both parents tucking me in. I woke up once and they were asleep together in the other bed, my father's arm around my mother. I thought about going over and crawling into bed with them but the next time I woke up it was bright morning and I was cozy in my own bed. But over many years I felt the loss of the last time the three of us could have been in one bed with our arms around each other.

They were sitting on the other bed drinking coffee. They had been sitting there together, watching me sleep.

CHAPTER

11

It was getting harder to say goodbye to Dunham each time he left. I didn't seem to have a family anymore when he went north to cook at the logging camp. I loved my mother but she was having another baby. And Jack and I could never be friends. And her spells. At school I was that polio kid from the nudist colony who was lousy at games. No one blamed me anymore but I was an outsider. I wasn't a Gerber either, fiercely as I had tried to become one. A patient gave Barbara and Lesley piano lessons but not me. Big Cathie was always making over their clothes but not mine.

Downstairs the clothes in my closet and my bed and hot water bottle all remained where I'd left them night before last but when I opened my big drawer I saw right away that someone had been playing with the doll the movie star Marion Davies gave me. Her dress was mussed and her hair had been combed. She looked better. Softer. More human. I called her the stranger doll and had never even touched her the whole year I'd lived here so why did I care if someone combed her hair? I cared because she was mine! The doll embarrassed me. She was almost as tall as I was and wore a red silk dress with lace at the neck, a rich untouchable stranger like Marion Davies herself had been. I'd only met her the one time she gave me the doll. I was three and couldn't walk after having polio but I'll never forget what she said to my father.

"She's such a pretty little thing. What a tragedy she's crippled for life."

There was no way I could love her doll. However, I would walk if it killed me. She was just a dumb movie star. Barbara wanted that doll but she was mine. Barbara had her whole family and piano lessons too. No one ever called her the polio kid from the nudist colony, did they?

"Barbara, did you play with my doll?"

"So what? You never even take her out of the drawer, poor kid. She'll go blind."

"That's the stupidest thing I ever heard. Dolls don't see. I'm gonna tell."

"Tattle tale tit, your tongue shall be slit. You tell on everybody!"

That stopped me. Did I? Did I tell on her? We stood there glaring at each other. Barbara loved dolls. This was the only one I'd ever had. I didn't play with her but that was my business, wasn't it?

"Girls!" We looked up to see Big Cathie at the stairway door. "I need Barbara to peel potatoes and Ella to pick berries, please." She didn't ask what was wrong and neither of us told her. The struggle over the stranger doll, forever nameless, raged on and remained our secret for months.

MEANWHILE, ACROSS THE ALLEY Carl finished painting the inside of Hugo's house for my mother and the expected baby. Marion would be staying in San Luis near the hospital until the baby was born. I wondered why but she wasn't around to ask.

Finally, my brother Peter was born on September 28, 1935. Jack brought them back to Oceano a week later, settled them in Hugo's house, and left, much to my relief. I ran across the alley and pushed open the door. Marion was nursing the baby and smiling.

"Come meet your brother, darling."

I crossed the room and stared at the baby, the first baby I'd ever seen up close. He was smaller than baby goats I'd seen nursing. Made more noise nursing too. His eyes were closed. I reached out a finger to touch the tiny hand. Such soft skin. Gradually his hand gripped my finger. We were together. He opened his eyes and we looked at each other. My own brother. My family.

"Do you mind that he's not a sister?"

I shook my head. I looked at that tiny hand encircling my thumb. He liked me!

"My little brother." I leaned down to kiss his soft dark hair. Our mother put her arms around me and the three of us stayed together, loving each other.

"Yes," Marion whispered.

I listened to him nursing, mesmerized. Pete was newborn and helpless but determined to get that milk, already a survivor. "Doesn't it hurt?" I asked.

"No, Baby. You were a strong sucker, too. I'm glad I have the milk to give my babies. Someday you will be glad, too."

I didn't want to think about that. "What's his name?" I asked, moving back to stare at him again.

"Peter, after your grandfather."

I almost said I was glad his name wasn't Jack but didn't want to start her sighing again. "Pete. I'll call him Pete." I said.

AFTER PETE'S BIRTH I COULD hardly wait to get home from school every day, to run across the alley and watch my mother nursing Pete while I told her about school. Pete's diapers always seemed to need changing. I had no trouble working the safety pins because when my clothes were torn I pinned them back together with safety pins. I knew how they worked better than my mother did.

Marion sent their dirty clothes to the Wet Wash out of the money Dunham sent to tide her over. Wet Wash was a pick-up and delivery laundry but they neither dried nor folded the clothes. When they'd come back clean and wet, Marion would often only move the sack to the closet instead of hanging the clothes outside on the line. Then they'd mildew. Barbara Gerber and I got in the habit of hanging the wet wash on the line and taking the clothes off before the fog rolled in so I'd have diapers to change Pete.

Marion also sent me to Angelo's grocery store and I'd bring back her order in my red wagon. Carl Angelo read her list aloud. "Cigarettes and canned fruit cocktail? These aren't on the list for people on relief. You're supposed to get cornmeal, raisins, nuts, and flour so she can make pancakes."

"She never uses cornmeal. My mother doesn't cook."

Mr. Angelo sighed and reached under the counter for cigarettes and pulled canned fruit cocktail off the shelf behind him. He gave me everything she asked for but he always grumbled first.

ONE NIGHT TOWARD THE END of November when I went across the alley to say goodnight to Marion and Pete, Jack was there, drunk. He and my mother were arguing. Pete was whimpering. The fire had gone out and the house was cold. I changed Pete's diaper and he had a bad rash. Marion had been forgetting to change his diapers lately. I wrapped him in a blanket and sat down with him at the end of Marion's bed.

"You promised I could live here. With you." Jack hissed the words.

"Only if you stopped drinking. Look at you!"

"I thought you loved me."

"If you loved me you wouldn't drink like you do." My mother's voice was quiet, weary, firm.

"So that's it, then." Jack stood there a while, staring at the three of us sitting on the bed. Suddenly, he picked up the kitchen chair he'd been sitting on and heaved it through the window behind us, shattering glass all over us. My mother slowly got up off the bed and faced him, glass shards falling off her.

"No, you don't," she said quietly. "Get out, Jack."

"I could hate you!" Jack screamed. Then, very slowly, he leaned back and socked my mother smack on the jaw. I heard his fist impact Marion's jaw. He turned and walked out. The door slammed so it shook the house. Then I heard his car start, his tires screech as he raced down the dark alley. I brushed glass splinters off Pete and myself.

"Are you all right, Baby?" Marion asked. There were tears on her face.

"Is he gone?" I stared at her. I'd never seen a grown-up hit another grown-up before. My mother's jaw was red and starting to swell.

I lay Pete down on the bed away from the glass and went to her. Marion put her arms around me and kept saying, "Ah, my babies, my babies," over and over.

"I'm going to get Rudy," I said finally, moving out of her arms.

"He'll say he told me so. But he's right. I can't marry a violent drunk." She began muttering about her mother and Hitler and communists and all the killing in the world in the strangest talking-to-yourself voice. I would come to recognize this as her going-into-a-spell voice. She didn't seem to know Pete and I were there. I picked him up and went for Rudy.

"A GOOD THING THIS HAPPENED before Jack moved in and got you pregnant again," Rudy said, opening his medical bag and sitting down next to Marion. He'd already swept up the shattered glass and put Pete in his crib where he'd gone out like a light.

"Oh, Lordie, Lordie, Rudy," Marion groaned as the doctor cupped her chin in his hand and, with his fingers, felt for broken bones.

"I'll be done in a moment if you'll hold still. Looks like your luck's held. Nothing broken. No crack in your jaw or your nose."

"She looks all black and blue," I said.

Rudy covered one side of her face in salve, snapped his bag shut and stood up.

"Ella, can you stay here and take care of your mother and Pete tonight? I'll come over first thing in the morning."

"Sure, if you'll write a note for me to take to school tomorrow."

I DIDN'T SEE JACK AGAIN that winter. Marion said Jack's temper was like her mother's. She said my grandmother would padlock the refrigerator between meals and also pushed her down the stairs.

Marion's depressions got worse. She began spending most of the day in bed. I thought her staying in bed was creepy but I did love to come home after school and go across the alley and tell her about my day. She always had time to share any problems, help with my math, listen to anything I wanted to say. My mother was a perfect listener unless she was deeply in a spell.

Rudy heard that Jack had taken up with a woman he worked with in the fields. Then we heard they'd moved in together. Then we heard she was pregnant. I was relieved when they moved to Los Angeles but my mother was sad. Marion stuck to her bed that winter but she did take care of my brother. Barbara and I hung out the wet wash. I did the shopping in my red wagon.

CHAPTER

12

I first met Esther the night she and Gavin arrived at the Gerbers' with four packages wrapped in gold paper with big red bows. We'd never seen such presents. They'd given the three Gerber girls and me each a Teddy bear, cuddly and with joints, our softest friends, the first stuffed animals I remember any of us having. Barbara's bear was yellow and Lesley, Cathie, and I got brown bears. We loved those bears more than people.

Esther had been married to Evelyn John St. Loe Strachey who was in the English Parliament before she married Gavin and she loved politics and what my mother called the movers and shakers. She stood over six feet tall, had a mannish haircut, and was the first woman in Oceano to wear high heels and tailored pants. Big Cathie said she was handsome rather than pretty. Esther moved into a house Gavin was renovating but Oceano bored her. She must have been really desperate to stoop to discussing the national and international news with me, a seven-year-old, but I loved hearing her

British accent and watching her nod as she'd glance at each book I'd taken out of the Halcyon library.

I'd stop by on my way back from the library and knock. Esther was usually reading and had a whiskey. She'd stand up and get me a coke from a tiny refrigerator in the wall behind her. She'd put ice cubes (they were the only ice cubes in Oceano) in a tall glass and hand me the glass and the coke.

"Cheers," she'd taught me to say and we'd touch glasses.

We sat across a table in this huge book-lined living room, overlooking an apricot orchard and facing straight out to the sand dunes in the distance.

"Show me what you're reading," she'd say and I'd hand her my stack of books from the Halcyon Library.

After she handed my books back, Esther flipped on the radio to the afternoon news. We listened. She taught me to listen carefully by asking many questions after the news was over.

Esther taught me to evaluate the news, "to reserve judgment" until I could figure why politicians were saying what they did, and she gave me a lifelong interest in how governments work.

Aside from my mother, Esther was the first person I heard say a world war was "impending."

Dunham had a bad attack of the malaria that had plagued him since his chain gang days. He wasn't in Mendocino anymore. He was in New York so he couldn't come to see me, but he wrote twice every week. Somewhere, he'd gotten a typewriter so I no longer needed Winonah Varian's translations. Instead I shared his letters with Esther because she was so comforting. She always said he was as good a writer as any of her famous friends in England. Winonah thought it funny that he wrote to me as if I were a grown-up. Esther thought it meant he loved me and considered me his equal, that he enjoyed talking with me.

THAT SAME WINTER RUDY'S stepmother's widower, Fermin Sepulveda, moved next door to my mother and Pete. Fermin was a Yaqui Indian who was a shaman and had the gift of water divining. Because of his accurate water divining he was one of the few people in town who was paid in cash. Fermin's wife, who had been Rudy's stepmother and a famous opera singer, had died the year before and he was lonely. Rudy had told us that Fermin had had a dream some years ago that he was to go to a certain house and ask the woman inside, whom he'd never seen, to marry him. The next morning he did. That was how Fermin and Rudy's stepmother met and married.

Fermin didn't see why this shouldn't work again. He promptly proposed to my mother and took over the care and feeding of Pete. He made an Indian carrier and hauled Pete around on his back. I was so happy to have Fermin taking care of Pete. Unfortunately, my mother thought Fermin enjoyed Pete for his own sake and she had no romantic interest in a man old enough to be her father. I reminded her that he was not only Indian but a shaman and a thousand times nicer than Jack.

"Oh, Lordie, Lordie, haven't I had enough of all that," she'd say to him.

"You'd never have to worry again, Marion, either you or Petey."

"Enough is enough, Fermin. Never again. I mean it."

Fermin Sepulveda: a savant who had been Rudy Gerber's stepmother's husband.
Courtesy of Dr. R. W. Gerber Family Papers.

After Fermin left that afternoon I reminded Marion how good Fermin was to Pete.

"Baby, you and Petey are my babies, not his. Remember our family. That's what I do." She put her arms around me and hugged me. Somehow, after that I didn't bother her so much about Fermin, though my hopes hadn't faded.

In spite of romantic incompatibility, my mother and Fermin became and remained the closest friends. While Fermin cooked for Marion and cared for Pete they talked hours every day. I loved to listen when they talked about their childhoods, his in Mexico and hers in Flatbush. Or their marriages, Marion's to my father and Fermin's to Rudy's stepmother.

ONE AFTERNOON THEY CHANGED my life. Fermin and Marion began reading aloud to each other about the Theosophical beliefs in Halcyon. They'd both been raised Catholics and were comparing beliefs. I'd been baptized Episcopalian but knew nothing about faith. Neither the Gerber girls nor I were raised in any religion. I was curious. The only people we knew who were religious were the Theosophists.

"Creeds disappear. Hearts remain." Fermin quoted the Theosophist saying.

"Ah, but the heart of a Catholic is fierce. As a child I yearned to be a nun. The pull was that strong," Marion said, shaking her head.

"Yes, yes, I know, but reincarnation makes sense. God uses trees and fish and water over and over. Why not use us, at least our souls?"

"Fermin, what do you mean?" I asked.

Marion explained that reincarnation meant a person lived seven lives getting rid of bad karma and becoming a better human being with each life.

Two days later I was pumping on the swing Fermin had made me in the vacant lot's eucalyptus tree when I realized what they'd been saying. God could use my same old soul in each of my bodies in different lives. Everyone's souls. We'd just go on and on. The soul kept learning. Why not? It was such a powerful and joyous jolt that I still think of that moment as a spiritual awakening.

CHAPTER

13

In January of 1936, my spiritual awakening was sorely tested when Rudy drove back from an old patient call in the dunes and told me that Arther Allman was dead. I was stunned. How could God let Arther die? He was my best friend.

Doggett and Hugo walked up from Moy Mell to the Gerbers' the afternoon before Arther's funeral. The other Dunites would join us early in the morning. It was sunny and clear and warm for a winter day. Rudy was keeping Barbara, Lesley, Cathie, and me busy begging flowers from the neighbors and picking the first wild mustard in the fields. Then Big Cathie helped us arrange them in Mason jars with water. We would leave them on the grave because Arther loved to paint flowers.

Carl would bring a blanket of morning glories. He said he wished he could bring up the yellow evening primrose, Arther's favorite dune flower, the flower he said followed Dunites when they left and sprung up in their

Arther Allman,
sculptor and writer.
Courtesy of Dr. R. W.
Gerber Family Papers.

flower boxes, even in New York City.

"She'll help her friend Arther pass," Marion said gently. My mother was taking me to the funeral to say goodbye.

"Our girls aren't going," Big Cathie said firmly. "They haven't known Arther that well and it might give them nightmares." We were sitting around the kitchen table after dinner and everyone looked at me. I'd be the only child and we knew Big Cathie didn't think I should be going.

"He and Ella were so close. Best friends." Marion sighed.

"Your best friend was an old man?" Lesley asked in horror.

"Arther's really dead, like a rabbit?" The question burst from me. I didn't answer Lesley.

Marion sighed again. "He'll live on in our hearts and our memories, Baby. Don't you worry."

"But if Arther died, how about Doggett and George?"

"Everyone dies eventually," Rudy said. "My job as a doctor is to keep them from dying before their time."

I looked at Rudy and then around the table. No surprised looks. They all knew everyone died. I'd seen dead sea lions, seals, and birds on the beach but I'd never seen a dead human being. Why would God kill everybody?

Did he? I didn't ask because I didn't want the Gerber girls to laugh at me. They seemed to know all sorts of things kids were supposed to know that I didn't. They looked like they knew about dying. How come nobody ever told me? Was I just dumb or was this one more thing—if it was even true—that you only learned from other kids?

"Will I have to see Arther dead? Hard and stiff like a sea lion?" I said, when I saw that Barbara was looking curiously at me. Did she guess I hadn't known about dying?

Big Cathie answered. "No, the casket will be closed. Don't worry. The Dunites will just take turns saying nice things about Arther."

My mother was counting her rosary beads. She'd been raised Catholic and so sometimes she'd tell me about God. I'd heard Rudy say Marion should give a blessing at the funeral since both she and Arther were lapsed Irish Catholics. I didn't ask what lapsed meant. Probably everybody but me knew that too.

WE WERE GATHERED AT THE cemetery the next morning and a Catholic priest in long black robes was shaking incense over Arther's casket when I suddenly began to think about dying. The casket was covered in the blanket of the first morning glories from the dunes and guarded by mason jars of flowers we'd picked yesterday. I was the only child.

"Arther was a man of adventure." Rudy spoke loudly. "He started life as the fourth son of an Irish baronet. He's been Vice Admiral of the Ecuadorian Navy. He saved a Tibetan nobleman in Nepal from drowning. He was a talented artist and my oldest Dunite friend. This is a man who lived well!"

Marion and the priest had both said something in Latin that Carl told me meant rest in peace, which he was sure Arther would. After all, he'd always slept well. Marion and Doggett were both crying and other people were wiping their eyes with handkerchiefs.

But I was remembering Arther making me cocoa, until suddenly I saw every single person at the funeral dead and lying in caskets, one after the other. Even me and Marion. Rudy said everyone dies! But that wasn't the worst. Dunham might die in New York and I'd never see him again! New York was a place where millions of people died. I began to cry. Why did Dunham go and leave me, anyhow? He left me so he could die in New York. I would never see him again.

Then I screamed. I became hysterical. I stamped my feet. I kicked dirt. I hit my mother.

"Poor Baby. Arther was your good friend," Marion whispered, trying to hug me.

"We should have left her home," Rudy said.

"Shut up and listen, Ella. You can cry later," Carl said.

The gravediggers finished shoveling out the grave. Half a dozen Dunites lowered Arther's casket into the ground. I stood by my mother, screaming, in agony because I was seeing my father lowered into that ground.

"You made Dunham go," I yelled at my mother "You and Jack."

"No, Baby, family pride and Upton Sinclair's defeat sent him back to New York."

Rudy hustled Marion and me away so other people could say goodbye to Arther in peace. Still crying, I must have walked across the graves of a hundred people but all I could think about was never seeing my father again. Still, eventually, my screams subsided to sobs and finally into an exhausted blubbering.

"Marion, if Dunham dies in New York, can we have his funeral here?" I finally managed to ask.

"Oh, Lordie. Your father isn't going to die in New York. Dunham said he'd be back for you and he will." My mother had tears in her eyes.

"But Rudy said everyone dies."

"Not any of us for at least fifty years."

"How will I know when it's fifty years?

"Your hair will be grey and mine will be white."

I stopped crying. Arther did have grey hair.

I KEPT THINKING ABOUT DYING long after the funeral. Dying was stupid. You finally make a friend and she dies. You spend all your life learning to read and write and play the piano and then you die and can't do any of it. People you love die and leave you alone. What was God thinking? My mother would know because she had wanted to be a nun when she was a child but somehow I couldn't bring myself to ask her. God was her friend and I didn't think much of his judgment.

Winter turned into spring and, though dying still haunted me, I was getting better at pushing it away. It was something I'd think about later. After all, I had fifty years. Meanwhile, I settled into school but looked forward to getting back to Moy Mell. I hoped Jack would stay in Los Angeles and never come back to the dunes. Never in his whole life. I prayed Dunham would come back real soon.

FINALLY, IN APRIL, SCHOOL CLOSED for Easter week. Oceano was a town built of shacks that had old cars disintegrating in front yards and its two hundred and fifty people scratching for their next meal. There was one main street, two bars, two corner groceries and hungry dogs wandering the streets. But in late April Oceano suddenly turned beautiful, with lupines and poppies blooming under a blue sky. The whole town looked carpeted in orange and blue the day Carl came to take me home to Moy Mell.

We had so much to catch up on. Carl said Moy Mell would be full of the old gang. Gavin's brother Loring and John Steinbeck had both written they'd be coming through. Edward Weston and his son, Brett, were due in to photograph the spring dunes any day now. That must be why Carl was carrying a gunnysack of vegetable culls from the packing shed over one shoulder. With our only car in New York, someone had to carry everything we brought from town.

"Dunham writes that he and Gavin will be back for my birthday, July 14, Bastille Day, you know."

"That should set off some fireworks."

"What do you mean?"

Carl flushed. "Oh, Bastille Day is the French 4th of July. Firecrackers and stuff."

"Dunham makes me strawberry shortcake for my birthday."

By this time we had reached the ramp to the beach and I ran down it, arms out. I started turning cartwheels. It was low tide so the sand was wet and hard. Perfect.

I ran ahead down the beach flapping my wings like a seagull taking off.

THAT NIGHT THERE WERE JUST Mary and Carl, Hugo, Doggett, my mother, Pete, and me around the bonfire. I missed Arther but I didn't miss Jack. Our clam chowder and cornbread was a feast. The sky was ablaze with stars and Hugo taught me more constellations. These stars had been the calendar for the Indians when they lived here. Hugo read his poems. We sang. Marion sat with her arm around me and kept giving me little hugs and smiling. I loved to see her face happy by firelight because of me.

THAT AFTERNOON COMPANY KEPT coming. Gavin's half-brother Loring, home from the South Seas, walked over the dunes with his ukulele over one shoulder. Edward Weston and John Steinbeck came in with a woman I'd never seen. Also Edward's eldest son Brett. I liked Brett but I hated to see him coming because it meant he'd go photographing with his father in the morning and I'd have to stay home. But John and Loring were welcome. Loring was going to teach me to play the ukulele as soon as my parents got enough money to buy me one.

John Steinbeck reminded me of my father. They were about the same height and build with brown curly hair and they both were rather quiet and had sudden great smiles. John's voice was warm like Dunham's when he read his stories. He wasn't famous yet but he'd published three books and that was more than anyone else in Moy Mell had done. My father did have three screenplays in Hollywood, newspaper and magazine articles published, and he was writing his first novel.

Carl and Brett went surf fishing and brought back enough perch for a feast that night. I fell asleep listening to Gavin's brother, Loring, play South Sea Island songs on his ukulele. Marion's arm stayed around me. She'd explained that Edward Weston and John Steinbeck's woman friend wasn't a vampire dripping blood. She was only wearing red nail polish, the first I'd ever seen.

"I used to wear nail polish when we lived in New York," Marion added wistfully.

"Ugh," I said.

"Your father liked it."

I was up early the next morning but I didn't go clam digging. I waited around in case Brett didn't get up and I could go out photographing with his father. Unfortunately, Brett got up.

"Now I've missed clamming with Carl and stupid Brett got to go with Edward," I complained, throwing myself on the daybed.

John Steinbeck looked up from the book he was reading. "I'm going over to talk with some hoboes. Want to come along?"

"Up the creek?"

He nodded.

"Sure."

"Well, go tell your mother."

"She won't wake up until lunch."

He gave me a look but didn't say anything. We left a note on the table so no one would worry about either of us and took off.

The fog was thick and low and emphasized by the mournful cry of a foghorn. We heard geese honking overhead but couldn't see a one. We walked down the beach until we came to the creek and then followed the creek back through willows toward town. I told John how Dunham used to get stuck here with our car Belinda. He'd haul Belinda to Halcyon and he and Russ Varian would take her apart and she'd run again until the next winter. John said Belinda sounded more cooperative than any car he'd had. John walked fast and it was all I could do to keep up with him, especially once we turned and followed the creek toward town.

The first I knew we were getting near the hobo camp was the good smell of coffee. And then something else that smelled really wonderful. "What smells so good?"

"You never had bacon before?" John asked, taking my hand.

I think there were six men around that fire. They looked startled to see us, even scared.

"We're out for a walk and it's cold. Mind if we warm up some?" John grinned and the men relaxed and nodded. A couple of them smiled.

"We thought you might be a cop," one man with a scruffy beard said.

"Never been a cop but I've been arrested," John replied.

"Want some stew?"

"Thanks. I'd appreciate some coffee. And my friend here has never tasted bacon."

"The first we've had in a good spell, too." The man who said this seemed younger than the others, maybe still in his teens, though he was so dirty it was hard to tell. But he was the only one who didn't have any beard.

I looked around. They reminded me of Dunites except these men were younger and dirtier and kind of gloomy. They'd hollowed out a place in the willows big enough for them to sleep and have a fire, and they were next to the creek so they could wash out their cups. Some leaned on a sleeping roll or a knapsack. John's coffee came in a washed out soup can. Their bonfire was mostly coals and the biggest Chase and Sanborn coffee cans were boiling over it. One can held coffee and the other had stew. The men would drink a cup of coffee and then put stew in their enamel mugs and eat that, then rinse the cup in the creek and dip out more coffee. One man was roasting strips of bacon on a willow twig and we each took off a piece with our fingers.

"I love bacon. Thanks," I said, even before tasting the crisp salty nuggety meat. The man roasting the bacon gave me another piece.

"Where you from?" John asked the man who'd thought he might be a cop.

"Arkansas, but I been riding the rails nearly three years now."

"Long time."

"Lost my job and headed out here to pick fruit but jobs ain't but few and far between."

"We get a few days once in a while is all. You got a smoke?"

John brought out a pack of cigarettes, opened it, and passed them around.

"Take two or three, for later."

"Thanks."

A guy in an old dress hat said he left a little girl like me because he couldn't feed her. I thought of the canning Dunham did before he left for New York and the money he sent the Gerbers to feed me and I felt sorry for that man's daughter. I figured the railroad station was about half a mile further into town. I wanted to ask how they snuck on the trains but thought maybe I'd better not. They must get on after dark.

I was restless by the time John finally stood up and rinsed out his soup can cup. "We thank you kindly for sharing your breakfast," he said, as we left.

"So, what do you think?"

I stared at John. "At first I thought they were like Dunites but they were so dirty."

"They might be happier if they were Dunites."

I shrugged. "My father said he rode the rails once and the cops caught him and put him in the chain gang."

"He never told me," John said.

"And I felt sorry for the kid whose father left her."

"Even if he couldn't feed her?"

"Now she doesn't have her father or food."

As we came out to the beach, John grinned and pointed out two shark bites on a sea lion carcass. Beyond, pelicans were diving into schools of perch. When we got back to Moy Mell John disappeared to write, which is what my father would have done.

I helped Carl peel potatoes for the clam chowder.

"Have a good walk?"

"I had bacon at the hobo camp," I said

"You know something, Ella," Carl said, flipping ashes and moving his cigarette from one side of his mouth to the other, "I am getting damn sick and tired of eating clam chowder."

"Get some bacon. Don't shoot any more swans. Poor Carl," I said.

14

One morning in May 1937 our third grade class at Oceano Grammar School was walking to Miss Freeman's house, something we had never done before.

We were going to listen to the Coronation of King George VI of England on the radio in Miss Freeman's living room, a room with a matching sofa and chair and a rug on the floor.

"Miss Freeman must really be rich," I whispered to the girl who was a rising leader in calling my mother the crazy lady.

"So what?"

I moved away from her as we sat down, most of us on the floor. Miss Freeman snapped on the radio, a brown wooden console, as tall as I was. Then we jumped up. The radio had started playing "America."

"No, children, sit down! That's 'God Save The King.' The music's the same but the words are about England. We don't stand up because America is independent now. Sit down!"

This Coronation took place before television was invented but we'd seen newspaper pictures and I'd saved seven allowances for a little tin box with two princesses painted on top. I'd been reading every word in my mother's magazines about Elizabeth and Margaret Rose for months. I listened intently as a radio reporter described King George VI and his queen leaving their coach. Then they walked on a royal red carpet all the way from the street to the nave of a cathedral that was banked in fragrant white flowers. I could imagine them in their purple robes, trimmed in ermine. I could as good as see their daughters and the Queen Mother behind them. The older one, Princess Elizabeth, would be Queen of England one day. They were little girls like us, except they wore silk dresses and white patent leather shoes. They were princesses in a fairytale. We adored and were in awe of them.

I was proud that my father was a British citizen, one of them. My great-grandmother Nannie was in London. Maybe she'd gone to the Coronation and was seeing it all, in real life.

The Royal Family sat on chairs and an Episcopal priest placed the crown on King George VI. Then he crowned Queen Mary. Soon they were walking back up the red carpet with the princesses behind them. Too soon they were outside getting into the coach. Did the girls take their grandmother's hand? The announcer didn't say. Maybe there'd be a picture in one of next month's magazines.

After the Coronation Miss Freeman gave us each a brownie to eat on our way back to school. She told us to walk in as straight a double line as possible—as if we were walking on that red plush carpet. We tried. We also played Coronation the rest of that school year. The biggest fights among the girls were over who got to be Princess Elizabeth, the future Queen, and who got to be Princess Margaret Rose, our own age. I don't think I was ever a princess but I was crowned the Queen once. I was so proud. We were all proud and a tiny bit gentler to each other that spring because of those princesses, even though they were across the sea in England.

CHAPTER

15

After school let out for the summer I moved from the Gerber home into a tent next to Marion's studio-house across the alley. I was almost nine but, though Rudy set up the tent and announced I was moving, no one asked me if I wanted to. Why was I leaving? No one seemed mad at me but they must have known I didn't want to move to a tent at Marion's. My mother did ask whether I wanted my own tent or a bed in the house. I chose the tent because I didn't want to change Pete's diaper in the middle of the night.

I still had my bed, closet, and big drawer with the Marion Davies doll inside, downstairs at the Gerbers' house, so I figured this move was a visit. Maybe Dunham didn't have the $25 a month to board me this summer. Couldn't someone have told me? I felt abandoned and there didn't seem to be anyone to ask why I was in that tent. Two loving and hungry white shepherd dogs had adopted my mother. They moved into the tent with me. I called them Queenie and Princess. We three bewildered souls settled down together. Sometimes I missed Dribbly but I knew Carl took good care of him.

A FEW DAYS LATER I came home from the Halcyon library to find my toddler brother running naked down the middle of the street. Pete was laughing. I picked him up and started home but as we got to the door Pete began to whimper and struggle to get down. I hung on. Inside I found our mother lying on the bed, magazines strewn around her, staring at the ceiling.

"Marion, wake up! Pete was in the street."

"Adolph Hitler is evil personified," she replied.

"Down! Let me down," Pete yelled.

"Marion, you're scaring Pete. Say something to him." I wanted to shake her, still thinking she was asleep, but I didn't dare let go of Pete. I kicked the bed. She stared at the ceiling. Was she dead? I began to cry and Pete, seeing his chance, slithered to the floor. He took off running.

Pete on his own. 1938.
Courtesy of Dr. R. W.
Gerber Family Papers.

"Down with communism, up with God," Marion shouted. Not dead then, I thought, grabbing a diaper and two safety pins and going after Pete. Fermin was away working, divining wells, so I ran across the alley to the Gerbers' holding Pete in my arms.

"Marion's dying," I told Big Cathie.

She knocked on the doctor's office door. "Ella says Marion's dying. Can you go over?" She put an arm gently around my shoulder.

"Emergency," Rudy said, seeing his patient out the front door and grabbing his medical bag. We ran back across the alley.

He stood looking down at Marion, who stared, not seeing Rudy either. He listened to her heart, took her pulse, and pinched her cheeks.

"Is she—dying?"

"No, no, Ella. She's in what we call a catatonic trance. Tomorrow, or in a few days, she'll be fine. You and Pete come on back to our place this afternoon. We'll pop some corn."

"Catatonic trance," I repeated, relieved. I could ask Marion what it meant later, when she came out of hers.

That afternoon was the first time Marion didn't recognize either Peter or me, but far from the last. Her trances would last a few hours or two or three days. We got used to them. She had another habit that came to bother me even more. Marion had started getting grey hair and she'd sit outside by the hour with a mirror pulling grey hair out, strand by strand. Sometimes she'd sing dance tunes as she pulled out her hair. I sat watching her, imagining how kids would hate me when I had a bald mother. I couldn't pretend I didn't know her. Everybody in town knew my mother. The crazy lady. The crazy bald lady?

I finally asked Big Cathie one afternoon why I was in the tent. She said I'd been sent over to Marion's for the summer to help with Pete. Fermin was working so I was Pete's only babysitter. He was an early walker and was learning to climb. He was a beautiful child, with blue eyes and golden curls. He was happily curious and into everything. He was filthy most of the time but much happier that summer than I was, struggling to keep myself respectably clean while living in a tent, struggling to keep up with my baby brother, terrified of Marion's trances, disgraced before the Gerber girls.

Marion was forgetting to send our clothes to the Wet Wash again. Fermin had taken over that chore but summer was his heavy work time and he was usually gone when the Wet Wash truck honked. I remember diapering Pete with newspaper. I took my own clothes back across the alley and washed them at the Gerbers'. Most nights I had dinner there, too. I'd go over about 5:30 and look hungry. Barbara said mostly I looked like I was ready to cry.

GAVIN ARTHUR WOULD COME BY our studio house periodically with a couple of beers. He and Marion would talk for hours about Moy Mell and the dunes, their childhoods, their favorite writers or their reincarnations. Gavin said again that *Dune Forum* had gone broke because of some evil he'd done in a past life. He hadn't yet discovered what he'd done but he was working on it astrologically. They laughed a lot and I listened as if they told fairy tales. Then, as Gavin got up to leave, he'd say in that aristocratic voice of his, "Marion, my dear friend, why won't you let us adopt the boy? My house would always be open to you. Peter would go to Yale under my personal guidance. You'd never be sorry."

"Oh, Lordie preserve us, don't say that, Gavin. My babies are all I've got." She'd reach for Pete or me and hold on for dear life.

I could understand her not wanting Gavin to take Pete away from us but why wouldn't Marion think of marrying Fermin to give Pete a "secure home"? Then Fermin would take care of all of us, at least until Dunham came for me. She'd still have Pete and Fermin promised he'd take care of him so we wouldn't have to. He cooked good Mexican food too. If Fermin was good enough to marry Rudy's stepmother, Isolde, who'd sung at the Metropolitan Opera, why was my mother being so picky?

Barbara Gerber heard other people were also turned down when they wanted to adopt Pete. They'd seen him running naked in the street during one of Marion's trances. Barbara noticed that no one talked about adopting me. "Not even Esther."

"I don't care. I don't want to be adopted." I didn't want to live at Gavin's

Catherine Gerber, Marion, Pete, Gavin Arthur and Hugo Seelig.
Courtesy of Dr. R. W. Gerber Family Papers.

but it did hurt that Esther never even asked for me.

"Well, you can't live with us forever, you know," Barbara said.

"Says who?" I wanted to live with the Gerbers until my father came back and took me to live with him. But Barbara's face had a strange expression. She was my friend, wasn't she? Didn't she want me around?

"I only meant you have your own family."

"So?" Did I? Everyone wanted Pete in their families. Not me. I was the girl with the crazy mother and the father who hadn't visited all winter because he'd had malaria again, whatever that was.

"Well, if you want to stay around me you'd better stop breaking into Flamore's doll house!"

"How is it breaking in if the door isn't locked?"

FLAMORE, THE DAUGHTER OF THE Guardian in Chief of the Halcyon Theosophist Temple was supposed to have been born an Avatar, like Jesus or the Sri Meher Baba. Instead she was born a Down syndrome baby. She was a couple of years older than Barbara and me, with a spooky squeaky voice. That summer her family had built her a palatial playhouse in the eucalyptus grove across from my tent. Her dolls lived much better than I did. Flamore left maybe a dozen dolls and all their household goods, clothes, and furniture there all the time so when she went home I'd go over and play house.

Barbara thought playing with Flamore's toys was dishonest and had a hunch her house was haunted, anyhow, but I couldn't give up my magic playing. I was afraid of Flamore and of the owls that lived in the trees above her playhouse, too. They were scary! And Barbara was usually right. Still, I'd never played house before. I loved every single doll and all their furniture and especially the delicate blue and white dishes, made in Japan.

ONE DAY, ON MY WAY to the Halcyon library, the sheriff stopped me.

"Ella," he said. "You better corral that mother of yours or I'm gonna send her to the nut house. Standing out in the street yelling about Hitler. What are you guys thinking of?"

I was terrified. My knees shook. I couldn't speak but must have nodded.

Maybe he'd scared me worse than he intended because he said, "Okay, just keep her quiet. She'll likely get over it."

I watched him drive off in the sheriff's car, his cowboy hat at a jaunty angle. I trembled. Somehow I managed to walk the block to Ella Young's house. The Irish poet was out working in her lily ponds, mud up to her knees, her long silk Celtic robe tied around her waist. I told her what the sheriff had said. She stood there quietly thinking.

"No, Marion isn't crazy. All she needs is a full time maid," Ella Young said finally, handing me a yellow water lily. "She has a poet's mind, more than one can say for that sheriff."

I'd never seen a maid except in the movies at Pismo. They wore frilly aprons. I could see how a maid would sweep floors and cook and wash, stuff Marion didn't think about, but didn't only rich people have them? I liked the idea, though.

When I reached Gavin and Esther's she invited me in for a coke.

I decided not to say anything because they already wanted to take

Pete away from us. Esther gave me a coke and sat down with her whiskey. Almost immediately, I blurted out what the sheriff had said and what Ella Young had said too. Esther's face looked sad.

"If Marion weren't saddled with the baby, her life would straighten out. Gavin says she was a delightful woman when she came. Beautiful." Esther blew out a puff of smoke. "Jack's gone. We'd take good care of Peter. Marion would be free to start over."

How about me, I thought, but said nothing. I pictured Marion and Pete laughing together. Why did Esther think my mother wanted to start over? I finished my coke and went on to the library. Somehow, after Esther, I didn't feel like talking about the sheriff or my mother anymore. I didn't even go by the Gerbers' for dinner that night.

"You're looking a little blue, Baby. What's wrong?" Marion asked.

"People talk too much, that's all."

She came and put her arms around me and rocked me a little. Then she stood up, pulling me up with her. "How about a fire?"

So she made a fire and we sang the lullabies she'd sung when I was a baby. We read Pete some picture books Gavin had brought. She even heated up some Franco American spaghetti for dinner. At times like these Marion was the best mother in the whole world.

WHEN MY FATHER CAME TO Oceano for my ninth birthday I could tell right away he didn't like my living in the tent.

"Not ten feet from the outhouse and any bum who uses it," he said. He arranged that I move back to the Gerbers' as soon as school started. Meanwhile we'd have a holiday together in the dunes. He'd gotten a new job. He'd be working for the WPA Historical Records Project. He and the poet Kenneth Rexroth and Jack London's daughter would be writing up the history of California.

"And I'll come live with you?"

"As soon as I can afford an apartment and find a way to manage the babysitting, Gooch. You know I want us to live together."

THE DAY AFTER MY NINTH birthday Dunham and I drove down to Moy Mell. As we cruised the beach slowly I felt like myself again. I always knew I was home as soon as I saw the ocean and heard its surf. Dunham would take care of me even if I couldn't live with him yet. Fermin would take care of Pete and Marion. He'd feed the dogs too, and send out the wash and hang it up and take it down before the fog came in. He promised and Fermin kept his promises. I took a deep breath of salt air and let one worry after another blow away.

This was a clear day and windy enough so a deep blue ocean was white-capped and choppy. Sand dunes were blowing too but they'd settle back, and the Indian clam mounds remained, hanging on to their roots through a hundred years of winds. Maybe I'd find some arrowheads. We drove through colonies of gulls and sandpipers. Pelicans skimmed the water, fishing for perch. Seals barked offshore. We were the only people on the beach. We were quietly getting used to each other again so I was surprised when Dunham spoke.

"Want to go for a quick swim?"

"Sure. Where can I change?"

My father looked at me and at the empty beach. "My young lady. Behind a dune, okay?" he suggested.

I pulled out my suit and changed behind a dune while he changed in the car.

Then we ran hand in hand to the ocean and dove in. After the first shock, the cold water felt good. I could swim well now and Dunham adapted to my shorter stroke. We struck out for deeper water beyond the breakers, then turned on our backs, backstroking and splashing each other. Above, a line of pelicans searched the sea for fish, gliding, shadowing, then leaving us far behind.

Too soon my father's familiar, "Had enough, Ella?" let me know we'd better get on our way to Moy Mell.

He got us each a big towel and, still in our suits, wrapped in our towels and each with a gunnysack of clothes over one shoulder, we turned in toward the dunes.

WHEN WE REACHED MOY MELL, smoke was swirling out of the community house chimney. That meant guests. My real dog, Dribbly, came running. He looked freshly bathed. Carl took good care of him. I wondered if he'd smell Queenie and Princess, the tent dogs, on me.

"I was hoping for a quiet time with you. It's been a while," Dunham said, regret in his voice.

"Yeah."

We walked in to find Carl, Edward Weston, his son Brett, and the Dunite poet, Hugo Seelig.

"Dunham Thorp!"

My Dad broke into his lopsided grin. These were some of his favorite people.

"And Ella, my best helper," Edward added.

"Can I go out photographing with you tomorrow?" I couldn't stop myself from asking, though his son Brett was right there.

"Better yet, we'll go in about an hour. As soon as I get my late afternoon shadows."

Edward was giving Carl some photography pointers so the three of us headed out into the dunes behind Moy Mell, Edward and Carl with tripods and cameras, me with a bag of plates. Carl and I trailed behind, letting Edward make the decisions. I wondered if Edward had told Carl to be quiet so he wasn't distracted from taking photos the world needed. Maybe Carl just knew. The sand felt warm between my toes and I found an arrowhead right off. I didn't say a word, just held it up. Edward kept looking around as if he already knew what he was hunting for.

Then he took Carl's arm and pointed. We were looking at a great sweep of partially shadowed wind sculpted dune. I yearned to scramble to the top and roll down. But I was Edward's helper and I didn't move. Edward and Carl set up their tripods over to one side, looking across the dune. Edward didn't say much to Carl. Mostly he'd point and Carl would look and then nod.

They worked until the sun hit the horizon. I was cold but I would have frozen solid before I said one word. Edward didn't need chatterboxes for helpers.

By the time we got home Dunham had cooked up a delicious goulash he called mess and rice. Fog came in so we sat around the fireplace eating and "catching up" as my father called it.

Dunham said he'd gotten sick and tired of cooking for thirty men in a logging camp. He was looking forward to the WPA Historical Records Project and writing the history of California. He'd about finished a rough draft of his novel. Edward said his prints had been selling through galleries, enough to keep his family eating. Carl loved photography and so he was content to wait out the bad depression times in Moy Mell so long as he could earn enough pulling cars out of the surf to buy himself film. Hugo wanted to know what his friends thought of "Wheel of Fire," his poetry book. I never found out because I fell asleep leaning against my father's knee, listening to the far-off cry of the coyotes and the steady pulse of the surf, and smelling sage and salt water on the wind.

When Dunham left two weeks later, he promised to figure out a way for us to be together.

"That's a promise. I'm waiting," I said, giving him a hug.

Rudy brought Barbara to Moy Mell when Dunham left and she stayed with Carl and me for a week. Barbara and I both look back on that week as the time of the *Iliad*, which Carl read aloud every day after we'd brought in enough driftwood for the fire. Carl said even the Greeks needed wood for fires. They weeded their gardens, too. I went clamming with Carl but Barbara didn't like clams so she squeezed orange juice instead. The Gerbers were vegetarians. We all liked beans, fortunately. At night Carl taught us to play poker. Both Greeks and Trojans gambled and Carl thought Barbara and I would have fit right in.

"Etgay ootay orkway," Carl would say in pig Latin every morning, pounding the gong. He said he was Agamemnon rallying his troops.

"Iyay amyay eefray." Barbara called back. She was free.

I started out wanting to be a general but Carl and Barbara said women weren't generals unless they were gods first. So I thought of myself as a beautiful Greek dancer who entertained the warriors between battles and on the long marches. I floated over the dunes. I wore the gold dust bracelet

Hugo had given me. I inspired whole armies.

Barbara was someone different every day. But she never became Helen of Troy because Helen and Paris touched off the whole war. They were capitalist warmongers.

Hugo told us the story of the final battle between Achilles and Hector and how peace finally came to Troy and to Greece. He acted out the battle and his low rich voice made the time come alive. "Remember that this story has lasted so long because it was written in great poetry," he would say as he wound up his story every night.

Somehow, between them, Carl and Hugo ended the *Iliad* the night before Barbara left. I stayed on in Moy Mell until I returned to the Gerbers' for school. Barbara would be in fifth grade and I would be in fourth.

16

I moved back to the Gerbers' home the day before school started. I was happy to fold my tent and move back across the alley to their warm and orderly life. I was ready to go back to school this year, too, but every afternoon after school I'd run across the alley to give my mother and Pete a rundown on my day. They listened intently, as if they were hearing a soap opera.

Barbara and I were in the fourth and fifth grade classroom this year, in a building up a little hill from the schoolhouse for kindergarten through third grade. Fourth graders could listen to the poems the fifth graders were memorizing. It proved a great incentive for finishing my fractions in a hurry. And I could hear Mrs. Northey read the fifth graders American history if I finished studying my spelling fast.

This year the three Gerber girls and I were all in school so every night after the dishes were done we sat around the big kitchen table doing homework. After homework was finished we could draw or move into the living room adjoining the kitchen. If there wasn't company we could sit in front of the fireplace and read. Often Rudy played his cello while Big Cathie read or helped with our homework. We all asked Big Cathie rather than Rudy for help because he was too apt to say our homework was idiotic. Or we were. Big Cathie had trained to be a teacher. She was gentle and explained what we didn't understand. At nine-thirty we had hot chocolate, filled our hot water bottles, and went downstairs to bed, where we could read until we fell asleep.

On Wednesday and Sunday nights we bathed in a round galvanized washtub filled with water heated on the wood stove. We each had five minutes or so to soap ourselves down, including hair, rinse off and step into a welcoming towel held by Big Cathie, smiling and with a geranium tucked behind one ear. Then the next girl felt the tub water, had more hot water added with a pitcher if it had cooled, and jumped in. We took turns for first, second, third, and fourth baths. Then we climbed into Dr. Denton knit pajamas with padded feet. How I loved the smells of the wood fire, incense, and Jergens soap on bath nights.

One night, as I was getting into the bath, I stumbled against the burning wood stove. I couldn't lift myself off. I screamed and screamed. The pain was searing, excruciating, the worst pain I'd ever felt. Rudy pulled me off the stove and into his medical office where he spread salve all over the burned shoulder and right side that had fallen against the stove. I sobbed inconsolably. All the time Rudy was working he bawled me out for being clumsy and careless and bawled himself out for forgetting that polio made me unstable. How was he ever going to explain to Dunham? How was he going to keep me from scarring? Some of it looked like third degree burns. He'd never play the cello while we bathed again. He'd stand there right next to us, between us and the stove, if the good God would only help me heal.

At first I cried but the salve Rudy used calmed the pain and I relaxed.

He'd also given me a shot that made me sleepy. I remember begging him to go on playing the cello while we bathed because I loved the music.

I wouldn't burn again. I'd stay away from the stove. I'd tell Dunham it was my fault.

So Rudy and I comforted each other. I was out of school for almost two weeks. Mrs. Northey, our teacher for fourth and fifth grades, came by and explained the assignments, including a special project we were to write on a person we admired. I chose President Roosevelt, because his voice was comforting on his radio Fireside Chats and because "Home on the Range" was his favorite song and mine too. My mother would bring Pete to the Gerbers' and help me with my report. I got to stay upstairs on the living room couch all day. I was in heaven. My burns were healing and didn't look like they would leave scars.

Then one day, when she'd promised to help, Marion didn't come over. We were afraid she might be in "one of her spells." I went over to make sure Pete was okay and found him asleep on the floor between the two shepherd dogs. I couldn't pick Pete up because of my burns so I ran for Fermin who, fortunately, had just gotten home to his house next door. He didn't know where our mother was but he took Pete home with him.

"Marion! Marion!" I yelled myself hoarse.

"*Basta*, Ella. She never hears in her trances and you're giving me an earache."

"But maybe the sheriff took her—or a kidnapper?"

"The sheriff would have taken her long ago if he'd wanted to and everyone knows she has no money to interest a kidnapper."

My mother didn't come home that night or the next day or the next. Fermin took Pete to work with him. None of us knew where Marion was or if something terrible had happened to her. I got a stomachache and started throwing up. Rudy put me in the car and we drove through town and met people who had seen her wandering around predicting a "huge war" but they didn't know where she'd gone.

Finally, after school on the fourth day, two young Jehovah's Witness men brought Marion home. They wore black suits, white shirts, and black ties, the first I'd seen. I thought they were policemen and was very relieved to discover they were not here to take my mother to the nut house as the sheriff had threatened. They were just nice men selling religious magazines who had found her sitting on a railroad track.

"I wish I had some beer to offer you," she said to the Jehovah's Witnesses.

"We don't drink, Ma'am. We can leave her with you, then?"

I nodded and they fled.

This was the first time our mother had gone walking in one of her spells. Unfortunately, her walks became something of a monthly habit. Nearly every time she'd wander off Jehovah's Witnesses would bring her home and wait until I came over after school. They must have saved her life more than once as they usually found her sitting on a railroad track. As I recall, she would be out of her trance when she returned, just a little bewildered, and after a day and a night of sleep she was her own gentle self again. It got so the neighbors started checking on Pete to make sure Marion was home and awake.

I don't know how much of our mother's illness my brother realized but I don't remember him being particularly upset about her disappearances. He only freaked out when she stared at him blankly. He was only about two when Marion started walking so it probably seemed normal. Fermin must have saved his life dozens of times. Even I rescued him a few times.

Once I remember coming into their house at dusk to find Pete standing on the kitchen table reaching for a box of cornflakes. He'd spilled the milk and was sloshing around in it, falling to his knees, as he reached toward the box on a shelf beyond his fingertips. We were lucky that the bottle hadn't broken. He didn't cry. He just wanted his cornflakes. I gave him the whole box, cleaned him up, and read to him until Fermin came home.

BY CHRISTMAS MY BURNS were a thing of the past. Even the scars were fading fast. Whatever Rudy did had patched me up once again.

On a cold winter day in February I was walking home from school with the brown teddy bear Gavin and Esther had given me. I'd been coughing, and had a sore throat and swollen glands in my neck. I'd felt lousy all day and taken Teddy to school for comfort. My head ached like crazy. Suddenly,

I realized that I didn't have Teddy. I doubled back all the way to school though I was terribly hot and my head was killing me. I needed Teddy. Where could he be? I'd just walked these paths and now I couldn't find darling Teddy. Where could he be? Where had he gone? He must be cold and lonely too.

At dark I finally had to give up and go back to the Gerbers'. The first person I saw sitting at the kitchen table was Carl. When he heard my story he took a flashlight and hunted for Teddy. Unfortunately, Carl couldn't find him even with a flashlight.

Meanwhile, Rudy diagnosed my fever, cough, and sore throat. "Whooping cough. The first case of the year and just in time so the whole town can have it by Easter."

"I've had whooping cough. I can take her to Moy Mell if you want," Carl said.

"It just might save us an epidemic," Rudy replied. "Though Ella got it somewhere, God knows. Still, it's worth a try, if you're willing."

He examined his girls but no one had symptoms. No one except me got to go. Nor were they willing to lend me their Teddies. Finally, Big Cathie made me a sock doll and Barbara promised to hunt for Teddy the next day.

Rudy drove Carl and me down the beach and then the two men carried me, wrapped in a down comforter, the quarter mile back into Moy Mell. Sick as I was I remember a full moon and a starry sky and the sound of the surf. I was home with Carl in the dunes. I felt better already. The smell of sage and eucalyptus and the purr of the surf comforted me. A coyote howled. Another answered.

Carl made a fire in the fireplace, lit the kerosene lamps, and we settled down with a story, this time a Zane Grey Western novel, though I fell asleep almost immediately. According to Carl I slept most of the next three weeks and woke up cured of whooping cough.

The way I remember those weeks, every time I woke up Carl would read me another chapter from Zane Grey. I loved his stories because I visualized the Southwest as an endless stretch of our sand dunes without ocean and their hills were rocky, not sandy. Carl said our sand was once rocks, so he wrote about our dunes long ago. Zane Grey wrote that the land smelled of sage and wind whistled through the canyons. They had coyotes and the bones of Indian tribes. There weren't so many horseback riders in our dunes but there were some. If Zane Grey could write about dunes, maybe—someday—I could too.

The only thing he got wrong was love. His hero and heroine loved each other forever and of all the people I knew only Big Cathie and Rudy were like that. Marion and Dunham didn't have a loving time together anymore and we'd once been a loving family. Almost everyone we knew was single. Carl said I should write and tell the author that but I kept falling asleep instead.

Only Carl and Hugo remembered they'd had whooping cough so they were my only company. They taught me Parcheesi and the three of us would play until I got a coughing fit. The other Dunites couldn't remember their childhood illnesses, though how anyone could forget the agony of coughing was hard to understand. Doggett would wave from the crest of a dune and come no closer.

I REMEMBER WALKING BACK UP to the Gerbers' with Carl one sunny winter afternoon. I was well and, so far as Rudy knew, no one else in town had caught whooping cough. I expected a warm welcome because Carl and I had averted an epidemic. What we found was most of the neighborhood in the Gerber garden watching Rudy and the sculptor Benny Bufano digging sludge out of the septic tank. Benny was even an inch or two shorter than Rudy, intense, powerful, and there was no mistaking the command with which he moved, even in a septic tank.

Everyone was talking. It sounded like a party. The plum and apricot trees were in full bloom. However, the stench was awful. Rudy was in the hole shoveling. Benny shoveled the shit on into buckets. He'd lost his right index finger in an accident but it didn't hold him back. Fermin was hauling away the buckets. Pete trotted along beside Fermin. The septic tank had overflowed again!

"Hello, Ella. Hi, Carl. Stinky, huh?" Barbara, Lesley, and Cathie called from the stairs.

Mr. Steffans, who lived next door, and Mr. Bernuti, from across the street, continued their game of chess at a table not ten feet from where Rudy and Benny were shoveling the smelly sludge.

The neighbors, most of whom had outhouses, were looking on with pleasure. People in the dunes and most in Oceano and Halcyon still used outhouses, so septic tanks with their flush toilets were the exception and they were glad to see them have trouble so they wouldn't have to put them in yet. However, everyone knew they'd have to install septic tanks eventually so they wanted to understand what had gone wrong.

Carl and I went on into the kitchen where Big Cathie was cooking up a big pot of beans for the extra people she knew would join us for dinner. Gavin Arthur was at the kitchen table drawing up Rudy's horoscope for the coming year.

"Rudy and Big Cathie have been invited to a conference of cooperatives in Salt Lake City this summer and he wants to know if they should go," Gavin explained to Carl. Gavin did horoscopes for all of us, whether we believed in them or not. I loved to watch him work with the colored pencils, drawing signs of the zodiac, the relation of the sun to the planets and the date and hour of our births. A startling number of his predictions came true.

"Catherine, I could have warned our Rudy this was a day he should have stayed in bed."

"I'm sure Rudy would agree, Gavin."

"You can tell that just by looking," Carl said, with a grin. "I'm going out to help."

"Not you, Ella. I need some potatoes peeled."

I wasn't too disappointed because I'd rather watch Gavin plot Rudy's horoscope than Rudy and Benny cleaning the stinky septic tank. But, within minutes Carl was back for towels. Rudy and Benny were in the outdoor shower and would be in for a glass of wine in five minutes.

It couldn't have been more than ten minutes before everyone was seated around the kitchen table, toasting the repaired septic tank and Benny's help.

"What is it with this man? Last time I dropped by, Rudy needed help shoveling manure for the vegetable garden and this time it's worse."

"You attract shit, Benny," Carl said and we all laughed.

"Never mind, this work builds my muscles for the ninety foot peace monument I'm going to build."

"That's going to take some ladder," Carl said.

As so often happened with the Gerbers, a catastrophe had turned into an excuse for a party. It was also true that for many years the sculptor did have a way of showing up to help just when Rudy had manure delivered or trouble with the septic tank. Whenever I see Benny's serene statue of Sun Yat-sen towering over San Francisco's Chinatown I remember him cleaning out the septic tank.

17

The spring of 1938 my father began writing me that he had almost enough money saved for the divorce. He wanted to know if I'd "given the matter any thought." Had Marion talked with me about where and with whom I wanted to live? Both he and Marion wanted me to be where I felt most comfortable. And, of course, I could always change my mind later.

What was he talking about?

I would be ten in July. I knew that divorce was a permanent separation. Sometimes families fought over money in divorce but my father had been sending money to Marion and $25 a month to the Gerbers for me, anyhow. My parents had separated a year—almost two years ago, when my father had Pretty Dolores and my mother had had Jack. What difference could a stupid divorce make now? Wouldn't I go on living with the Gerbers…unless they didn't want me anymore? Would I have to go back across the alley and live with Marion and Pete in all that misery and dirt? My stomach sank.

Kids at school called my mother the crazy lady of Oceano because she was always yelling about Hitler and communism being evil. I was the crazy lady's daughter. They weren't hitting me now but they had when they thought I came from a nudist colony and nudism was nothing compared to a crazy mother. If I moved back in with Marion they'd turn on me. When she went walking in a trance would I stay home and take care of Pete or spend the nights on the streets hunting for her? What would the sheriff do and what would happen to Pete and me if he "threw our mother in the nut house?"

Dunham didn't exactly ask me to come live with him but could you say that was what his letter meant? Or maybe not? I was afraid to let myself think so because I wanted to live with him so much. I was afraid to ask and have him tell me, "Sorry, Gooch, I have to work and there'd be nobody to take care of you." So I waited.

While I was waiting and worrying I was also fascinated by the home Gavin and Esther had been renovating and rebuilding for the last year or two on the hill between Oceano and Halcyon, the grandest house Barbara

Gavin and Esther Arthur at Hill House.
Courtesy of Dr. R. W. Gerber Family Papers.

or I had ever seen. Some people thought the construction meant Gavin had the expected inheritance from his uncle at last. Some thought this was Esther's money from her Mark Cross Leather inheritance. It was a hot topic because Gavin's house represented the only money in Oceano in 1938 and almost the only work. No one else we knew inherited money. There was that barony my father might inherit, but, as Carl said, you couldn't eat a title.

The great high-ceilinged rooms at Gavin's looked out over Halcyon, Oceano, and over the highway to the sand dunes that sheltered his old home in Moy Mell. There was a dining room with a table that seated twenty and an outdoor patio with a fireplace big enough to roast a pig. The living room, where Esther had her whiskey and I had my coke while she taught me politics, was now bigger than the Gerbers' whole house and the ceiling was twice as high. My stomach churned because I couldn't tell her my worries but it was still a comfort to be in that beautiful room with her.

Soon Gavin's grandfather's furniture arrived with the White House logo engraved on every piece and we felt like part of history. Gavin allowed the Gerber girls and me the run of his house, even though we were usually running with dirty bare feet. We especially loved playing billiards in the game room with President Arthur's private cue sticks, leaning against his presidential logo on the table. In fact, Gavin kept an open house while he decided whether or not to run for Congress. My mother said Gavin gave Oceano and Halcyon time out from the Depression. Hill House was better and cheaper than going to the movies.

Unfortunately, Gavin's friends still included Jack, who had gotten a job driving trucks between Los Angeles and San Luis Obispo. Barbara and I were forever running into him in the billiard room.

"How's Marion and the boy?" he'd ask.

"My mother and my brother are just fine," I'd say fiercely and turn my back on Jack.

"Go see for yourself," Barbara would say. "Ella, let's play billiards later." Then Barbara would pull me away before Jack and I could get nasty with each other. Barbara and I had heard grown-ups say Jack was Pete's father and though it seemed all too possible, I clung to the hope that he wasn't.

"Pete has blonde curly hair and blue eyes and Jack has black hair, brown eyes, and dark skin. Jack can't be his father."

"Go ask Marion," Barbara suggested.

"Why? What difference would it make?"

"Maybe he'd pay for Pete's food or get him some jeans."

"Oh, yeah? He's got another wife. Besides, Jack spends his money on whiskey." Ever since the night Jack broke the window and socked my mother I got sick to my stomach when I saw him. I was afraid he'd kill one of us. As far as I knew he hadn't been back to the house. "Wouldn't Jack want to see Pete if he were his father?"

"Some fathers don't like their kids," Barbara said quietly.

WHEN SCHOOL CLOSED FOR THE summer I tried to prepare myself in case the Gerbers sent me back across the alley to a tent like they had the previous year. When they didn't, I wondered if they knew what would happen to me when the divorce came through. Again, I wanted to ask but I was afraid to find out. I felt sick to my stomach all the time. I was ashamed to talk to Barbara about it. I felt disloyal to my mother. I couldn't talk to her about where I'd live after the divorce. She'd call me her baby and say I was all she had in the world and I'd feel so guilty there'd be no chance to live with Dunham.

My father arrived in Oceano a week before my tenth birthday. He didn't mention my custody. Neither did I. If he didn't bring it up after those letters I knew in my sinking stomach it was because he had to be away at work all day. There was no one to take care of me. This had always been why I couldn't live with Dunham.

The day after my birthday, Dunham and Marion and I drove up to San Luis Obispo to see the judge. Fermin took care of Pete.

Both my parents were nervous on the trip to San Luis. Maybe it was their clothes. Dunham wore a suit and tie. Marion had a clinging soft red dress and what she called a cloche hat. She wore make-up and perfume,

My parents' Hollywood wedding picture.

silk stockings and high heels. She was beautiful! Where did she keep these clothes? If only the sheriff could see her now! And the kids in school. I'd be so proud.

"You look so different," I whispered. "Pretty."

Marion emitted one of her deep sighs, then smiled, and put a hugging arm around my shoulder. "You'd like me to dress like this?" she asked.

"Oh, yes."

"Poor baby," My mother said. Then she lit a cigarette and rolled down the window.

"We know we're better off apart but I wish we could prepare her a little." It was the first time Dunham had spoken since we'd gotten in the car.

"Who? me?"

"Yes. You." He wiggled his ears.

"Prepare me for what? I know about the divorce." I suddenly felt rather important, coming to my parents' divorce.

"The judge just wants to talk with you after he's through with us," Marion said in a sad voice. "I'm sorry, Baby."

"It's okay." But I felt like throwing up. The judge was going to tell me where I would live and, guessing from Marion's voice, this wasn't going to be good news. The Gerber girls were still asleep and I was on my way to see this judge. It wasn't fair.

We'd reached the courthouse parking lot. My father switched off the ignition and we sat in the sudden silence together, maybe together for the last time. I felt tears and didn't want them. "What are we waiting for?" I pushed my mother and she opened the car door. She let me get out after her and then she leaned back in.

"Even so, there were good times, weren't there, Dunham?"

My father's face reddened. He looked mad. Then he shrugged and grinned sadly. "Don't you think it's a little late to be thinking about that now, Marion?" He turned to me. "Ella, are you going to be all right out in the hall by yourself?"

"I'll be okay." I held up *Heidi*, the book I'd brought to read.

Once they'd disappeared into what Dunham said was a courtroom, I sat on a bench along an endless empty hallway. I didn't open my book. I didn't imagine my parents with the judge. Maybe I felt like Marion did in one of her spells. Like nothing. I have no idea how long I was there. I only know that I came out of my blank spell when my parents opened that tall wooden door and walked over to my bench.

"Your turn, Gooch," Dunham said, rubbing my head affectionately. "Then we'll have lunch."

Marion buried her face in my shoulder. So I won't see her cry, I thought, pulling away a little from the tears on my sweater.

A policewoman came to take me back to the judge's chambers. He was waiting for me, she said. She had a sad smile too. I wanted to kick her.

The judge and I each had a coke and a melted cheese sandwich, just the two of us in a tall book lined room that reminded me of Gavin's house. He was easy and friendly, with a comforting grin like Dunham's. We'd been talking about the Gerber girls and about school, when suddenly he asked me flat out.

"Who would you really like to live with?"

"I'm too young to choose."

"Right, but it is your life. I'd kind of like your opinion."

I took a drink of my coke. "Choosing makes me feel like a rat." Did this mean I wasn't going to continue living with the Gerbers? Nothing was ever so good as living in the dunes with my father cooking meals and baking cookies and my mother singing and playing violin around the campfire. I couldn't choose that anymore. At least I could count on Dunham. He stayed the same, easy going and loving me. Marion was pretty scary when she didn't recognize me and walked all over town yelling. But why hadn't the judge said anything about Pete? Who was he going to live with? Dunham hadn't asked about him, either. I sat there a long moment, letting that sink in. Then I saw that the judge was waiting. I had to say something.

"My mother says she never met a broom yet she felt like dancing with," I said with a giggle. Shut up idiot, I told myself.

"Do you help your mother cook?" The judge bit his lower lip, maybe to keep from smiling.

"I help Dunham." I did keep myself from saying Marion didn't ever cook.

"Would you be more comfortable with your mom or dad, Ella?" The judge rubbed his hand over his eyes, like he'd asked too many kids this question.

I shook my head. No dice. But then I saw him gathering his papers together, folding his napkin, uncrossing his legs. This was my last chance. I remembered Mom on those four-day trances, walking God knows where and it was suddenly too much. If I was not around Fermin would take more care of Pete and he'd be safer.

"I'd rather live with Dunham." My voice was just over a whisper.

NONE OF US HAD MUCH to say on the way home.

"I'm the first in my whole family to have a divorce," my mother said. "We're Catholic, you know," she added putting an arm around me.

"It was better for Ella, with Jack in the picture."

"He's not anymore."

"Still, Pete's father."

So Jack was Pete's father. I wouldn't throw up. I wouldn't throw up. And then Marion startled me so I forgot about throwing up entirely.

"It's your English pride, Dunham. That damn barony."

"Marion—I gave Pete my name so they wouldn't write illegitimate on his birth certificate. What more do you want?"

"But you didn't want him in your family."

"He isn't in my family and shouldn't get Ella's inheritance."

"That pie in the sky." My mother snorted.

I was going to ask—what inheritance?—but then I remembered what I'd said to the judge and couldn't say a word.

My mother and I sighed.

18

The judge gave Dunham custody of me and Marion custody of Pete. I would live with the Gerbers during summer vacations because otherwise I'd be home alone. My father would be at work writing the history of California for the WPA all day. My mother had unlimited visiting rights.

"You'll finally be coming to live with me, Gooch." Dunham ruffled my hair and gave me a hug. I snuggled up to him. We were out in the alley, sitting in his car. "We'll be together in Berkeley by the time your school starts in September."

"For sure?"

"As sure as I've ever been about anything. At last we'll be together."

This was in July, a week after my tenth birthday. I kissed my father on the cheek. Goodbye, goodbye. Then I got out of the car as I had so many times before when he was leaving me. This time would be different. Dunham started the engine. I watched his old Dodge disappearing down the dusty alley. He was on his way north to Berkeley to find an apartment for us.

"September!" I shouted after the car.

I went over and sat on a bench in the Gerber's outdoor rock fireplace enclosure, hugging my knees, trying to figure whether I felt like laughing or crying. I'd wanted to live with my father forever and I wanted to escape my mother's crazy spells. But how could I live without her and Pete? How was I going to get along without the Gerbers, especially Barbara? I wouldn't see the dunes and the Dunites, not even Carl or Gavin. I'd never hear the ocean from Berkeley. And, as Barbara said, there were probably worse schools than Oceano. How could I face walking across another schoolyard where I didn't know one boy or girl? They'd all be strangers. Everyone I saw on the street would be a stranger. I'd be all alone until Dunham came home. But at least I'd be back here every summer. I could start looking forward to that.

The big thing was that I hadn't talked to Marion about my conversation with the judge, hadn't seen her since Dunham told me the custody decision. She must know I'd chosen. I needed to go across the alley and talk with her.

I looked at the watch Dunham had given me for my birthday. I had two hours before the Gerber girls and I had to head to Halcyon for the dress rehearsal of the annual Theosophists' Children's Play. I was going to be soggy white bread, the unhealthy food villain in a play about dancing vegetables. I had a big part. Big Cathie was finishing sewing my crepe paper costume at this very moment. This was the first sewing she'd ever done for me, and it made me feel like I belonged—at last—just as I was leaving the Gerbers.

I stood up. Better go over. What could I say to Marion?

My mother was sitting on a broken down chaise lounge in her back yard, reading. Pete was taking a nap on the other lounge. She set the book down, looked up, and smiled at me. "Poor baby, they made you choose."

I nodded. Marion's sympathy brought tears to my eyes. Maybe it wasn't all my fault.

"Daddy's girl. I was, too, as a child, and it was a good thing," she said. She held open her arms and I went to her. I cried and she rocked me and cried too. Then we lay there quietly together under the afternoon sun. I thought of Marion's mother. A mean grandmother I'd never seen. She'd hit my mother with a broom and pushed her down the stairs. Marion had never even spanked me.

"I've told you the story about my brother and me running away from home when I was sixteen. We went to hear Edna St. Vincent Millay read her poetry in Greenwich Village. I told her I wrote poetry too and we had no place to sleep. "You two can sleep here tonight. After all, we poets have to stick together," she said.

"You told me," I said.

But did I tell you how my father found us after a couple of months? "I miss you so," I can still hear him say those words and when he asked us to come home, I didn't hesitate. My father, after all. So I understand, Baby."

"I didn't want to choose. I'll write every week," I said. Another thing. I'd miss Marion reciting poems to me.

"Your letter will be almost as good as a visit. Tell me everything. And we still have the summers. In another few months Petey will love the train. We can take the train to Berkeley and visit you."

"I'll miss Pete," I said, realizing the words were all too true. My pudgy little smiling brother. Nothing stopped him. He hardly ever cried. He had a smile for everyone. I looked over at him, peacefully asleep, his behind scrunched up. He could sleep anywhere. Just last month he climbed up and took his nap on the top of Rudy's car. We were hunting for him all afternoon.

"He'll miss you, Baby. He loves to tease you."

"But he's way too fast for me. When I think he's napping he's out of bed and running down the middle of the street, flapping his arms like a seagull." I was afraid I'd get him killed someday when he was teasing me.

"He'll be talking a mile a minute when you come back. Dunham said he'd try and bring you down for Christmas vacation."

*Pete lost and found on
the roof of Rudy's car.*
Courtesy of Dr. R. W.
Gerber Family Papers.

Before I could answer we both heard the Gerber cowbell. Big Cathie was calling me home to get to Halcyon for the dress rehearsal.

I took off flying. My mother didn't blame me! "Hooray!"

AN HOUR LATER I STOOD with the Gerber girls and the children from the Theosophist community in Halcyon in an old building called Hiawatha's Lodge. Twenty of us rustled proudly in our crepe paper costumes and lined up in a double row to begin our first song. The play dealt with good and bad foods. Barbara was a tomato and Lesley was an ear of corn but I liked being soggy white bread, a villain with ruffles. Flamore, the Down syndrome child, whose father was the Temple Guardian in Chief and whose playhouse I loved using, stood directly behind me. She was Molly Milk. She'd come to other rehearsals but hadn't spoken or sung.

This time, when the rest of us sang, Flamore opened her mouth and sang too. I giggled. I was tense and hurting over my custody and couldn't help it. She sounded like an old elephant seal. The director, Winonah Varian, frowned. She was the lady who'd helped me decipher my father's handwritten letters and helped me choose library books, and I liked her. I tried to control myself. But, instead, I burst out laughing. I'd heard Flamore speak, a gruff horsy squeak, but I'd never heard her sing. Maybe I was atonal but her voice was a hundred times worse than mine. Also, she was so much bigger than the rest of us that she even looked like an elephant seal. The more I tried to stop laughing the worse it got. Barbara gave me a fierce warning look.

Winonah had Barbara take over because Barbara could take her place playing the piano. Then Winonah beckoned me to follow her. We went next door to the temple. The Temple of the People was a graceful octagonal white stone building with Greek columns surrounding a sunlit interior. I stood in a pool of light and felt peace seep all through me. Since our family were not Theosophists I'd only been inside the Temple a few times and never when it was empty. Marion said that the temple was designed to ease one into another life. "Creeds Disappear, Hearts Remain" was the motto. The heart must be pretty close to the soul. Death hadn't felt as terrifying since I'd heard my mother and Fermin talking about reincarnation. But there were a couple of things I still wanted to understand.

"What the hell is wrong with you? You hurt Flamore's feelings," Winonah said.

"Flamore's wrecking the whole play."

"She's doing the best she can. No one else is laughing, are they?"

"They're laughing inside."

"You're not usually mean. Has something upset you today, Ella?"

I shook my head. My custody was my business, not hers. I felt like saying everyone should have howled like Flamore but decided to change the subject. "Winonah, do I have to reincarnate into different animals before I can be reincarnated to a person?"

"Ella, we don't believe humans have animal lives. You may have been a boy, though. But, to get back to Flamore, what made you laugh? You know she tries harder than any of you."

"She wrecks everything. She's spooky."

"Nonsense," said Winonah, taking a long drag on her cigarette. "She was born that way. She can't help herself and she loves being in the program.

And maybe she'll improve, like you and your limp. If you keep laughing, I'll have to send you home and then we won't be able to use you next year."

"I'm moving to Berkeley in September, anyhow."

We stared at each other. I felt dizzy. Maybe I was going to faint.

"Since when?"

"Dunham told me this morning."

"And Marion?"

"They're divorced, you know. She has Pete."

"But she needs your help with Pete."

There it was. I felt like Winonah had socked me in the stomach. I groped for a chair and sat down. This was too hard. Why me? Because I chose to live with Dunham. I stared at Winonah and she sighed.

"Sorry. I keep forgetting you're only ten years old."

Winonah had been divorced and remarried and had custody of her daughter, Joan, a year younger than me. I could see the questions come crowding into her face but I shook my head. I wanted to tell her I'd be back summers but I couldn't get the words out. I started to shake.

Winonah put an arm around me. "I'll miss you like crazy. We all will."

We sat there in the sun-stroked quiet of the temple for a few minutes, then Winonah jumped up. "Let's make this the best damn program the Temple's ever done. So you can remember us." She pulled me up and we ran back to Hiawatha's Lodge and Flamore. I could only remember her words. "But she needs your help with Pete." I felt like soggy white bread. Even my crepe paper costume had wilted. I didn't laugh at Flamore. There was no more laughter in me.

19

Gavin had come by the Gerbers' to invite everyone to a party in Moy Mell celebrating the opening of Edward Weston's new gallery show. Ella Young would read from her fairy stories. Hugo Seelig would read his poetry. All the Gerbers and Marion and Pete and Fermin were invited. And all the Dunites, of course. His wife, Esther, was visiting in London so Gavin thought it was time for a Moy Mell party.

We were sitting around the Gerber table when Gavin turned to me. "Well, Ella, would you like to come to Moy Mell and help Carl and I set things up?"

I looked over at Big Cathie, peeling potatoes, a hibiscus flower over one ear. She nodded.

"Sure, when do we leave? I always want to go to Moy Mell."

"You're a true Dunite. Go get your things together. We leave in half an hour, to catch the tide."

I heard the four o'clock train whistle as we bumped down the ramp to the beach. The sky was clear and the ocean a dark blue. Seals brayed beyond the surf. I inhaled the smells of ocean and fish and sage and fresh air. Then I turned and looked back over the dunes—at wind sculpted sand and Indian shell mounds as far as I could see.

"Don't forget us, going up north with Dunham."

"Moy Mell is my home—forever!"

"That's the girl," Gavin said.

Aussie Slim, whose shack was our marker for turning in toward Moy Mell, had died a few months before and someone had burned his house down. Nothing was left but ashes. Not that I'd miss Slim exactly. He was scary and I'd always run from him. But I would miss the shack with the abalone shell roof and windshield windows. Gavin and I stood looking at the ashes and then he took my hand and we started back toward Moy Mell.

"I wonder if Slim's family knows he's gone," Gavin said.

"Does he have a family?"

"He never mentioned them but everyone has parents and most people have brothers or sisters, too. You and I do."

Postcard photo of dunes, Oceano, California.
Courtesy of Lesley Gerber Benn.

THE NEXT MORNING, MY DOG and goat and I went next door to Doggett's cove for breakfast. George Blais and Doggett were sampling George's home brew in their coffee when I arrived. They were in high spirits. George was brewing his wheat liquor for the party. It was foggy so Doggett and I were wearing jeans and heavy sweaters. George wore nothing but his loincloth. Someday I was going to tell George the trouble he caused me at school and in Oceano, how everyone thought we were a nudist colony because of him. But why couldn't he wear just his loincloth or nothing if he wanted to? Gavin said George was the oldest and the healthiest man in the dunes.

Once Carl saw my birthday watch, he put me on a schedule. The mornings were mine but from noon until three I was his helper. That afternoon we cleaned the kerosene lamps. I had gained the privilege of washing the glass chimneys and trimming the wicks while Gavin told us Indian ghost stories.

People started drifting in a day or two before the party. Edward Weston arrived with his sons so there was no hope for me to go out photographing with him.

So I helped Gavin. He had done some baking and we made a washtub full of stew. I liked peeling carrots and potatoes and celery. As Carl said, Gavin enjoyed every herb, every seasoning, every taste. He added wine to everything and shared his tasting with me.

Fermin brought Marion, Pete, Krishnamurti, and Ella Young at about noon on the day of the party. All afternoon people kept coming. When the Gerbers arrived I had to show Barbara, Lesley, and Little Cathie everything we'd done. Then Hugo introduced Hollywood movie friends who'd come north for his reading.

At dusk Ella introduced Hugo. She'd been collecting his poems, but Hugo wouldn't let her disturb Beady Eyes, the pack rat who had taken some of his poems to build his nest.

"Immortal poems were lost to a pack rat's comfort. Hugo has a true voice, mysterious and—"

At this point my mother came running into the community house.

*Ella Young, Irish poet
and fairytale writer.*
Courtesy of Peggy Weedon.

"Has anyone seen Petey? I've looked everywhere and it's getting dark."

"Marion, he's fallen asleep on one of the beds somewhere," Gavin said impatiently.

"Where? No, I looked. He's lost, Gavin."

Carl saw Marion's tears and took charge. "Look, it's time for a stretch before we hear Hugo's poems. Let's go find Peter."

He organized search parties, even sending people out to the beach, though how a three-year-old could go that far, no one except me could imagine. Doggett went back over the willow ledge to search his cove. Marion and Fermin and Barbara and I yelled our lungs out, calling him to come back. I should have looked after Petey. Marion needed my help with Pete, like Winonah had said.

After an hour or so, when Pete was still missing and it was truly dark. My mother had been calling Pete so loudly her voice began to give out. Everyone was worried. I was sick to my stomach. It was dark enough so that people were using flashlights and kerosene lamps and lanterns, cold enough for coats and jackets. Pete had only a T-shirt.

Rudy told about finding Pete on the top of his car.

"A three-year-old who can do that could be anywhere, five miles in any direction," Edward Weston said.

"He's likely fallen asleep by now," Fermin muttered. "He didn't get his nap."

"Behind any one of a hundred dunes," Gavin said gloomily.

"Poor baby, he's scared to death."

"He's hungry, Marion," Barbara said.

"We're all hungry," Carl said, "but no one eats until Pete eats."

The grow-ups went out in search parties, each with as many lights as they could find, and under strict instructions not to get separated and to check back every half hour in case he'd been found. Gavin ordered kids to stay in the community house so no one else would get lost. Marion was to stay with us so she'd be here when they brought Pete back. No one wanted to risk her wandering off.

I remember watching the torchlights make their way up the dunes behind Moy Mell. They seemed to float. The moon was nearly full and the sky was glowing with stars. The surf was heavy, pounding. The Indian shell mounds covered with clamshells shone white in the moonlight. Where would he go? Would the coyotes eat him? He was smaller than Dribbly and we used to worry about him. No, no, no.

Everyone was calling "Petey, Petey, come home." Or "Here Pete. Here, Pete," as if he were a dog.

"He only has a light shirt. He'll freeze overnight." Marion groaned.

If he doesn't drown, I thought.

We were kept busy boiling pots of coffee, to offer crews checking in.

Then, when we'd almost given up, when everyone was talking of going into town and getting the sheriff, I saw Gavin start running up the dunes behind Moy Mell. There was Fermin at the very top of the far dune, with Pete slung over one shoulder, waving his hat and a flashlight in an arc. He'd found my brother about a mile back in the dunes, at the edge of the creek.

"It's a miracle the kid didn't fall in." Rudy said what we were all thinking.

"Don't wake him. He needs healing," was what Fermin said, as he put Petey down on the bed next to Marion. She drew him to her and sang softly. Pete stirred but did not wake. I watched my brother, memorizing him. Even Fermin had lost him. But he found Pete, too.

"You found my baby," Marion kept saying to Fermin. "My little Petey. We lost him and you found him."

Carl blew the hunting horn, the agreed upon signal that my brother had been found. As each search group came in Gavin told them briefly what had happened and Carl handed each person a bowl of stew and a glass of George Blais' wheat liquor.

The party was underway. Gavin always said Pete was the making of his party. No one would ever forget the dunes or Hugo's poetry about them. But my mother says I wasn't the only one who fell asleep when Hugo read his dune poems at midnight. Pete and the rest of us slept late the next morning.

20

A couple of weeks later the Gerbers and our family stood around my father's old Dodge in the Gerbers' back alley. It was a sunny September morning. My gunnysacks filled with clothes were in the trunk, my bicycle strapped on the roof. Dunham and I were off on the Berkeley adventure, as my mother put it. She and the Gerbers were all there to see us off. Fermin carried Pete on his shoulders so he wouldn't climb into the car and come along. Neighbors leaned over their gates, offering advice. Down the alley fighting cocks crowed. Up the alley goats bleated to be milked. Rudy's Joseph's Coat roses were in fragrant bloom all along the back fence.

Dunham kept twirling his keys. He wasn't good at what he called interminable goodbyes.

I looked from him to my mother and wasn't surprised that she was sobbing. I bit my lip to keep from crying too. "I'll be back, we hope for Christmas," I promised guiltily.

"Don't forget, Dunham. She'll have stomach upsets the first few days eating meat after her vegetarian diet with us. Won't last long and it's not serious," Rudy said.

"Ah, poor Baby. We're tearing you in two."

"Getting schmaltzy, Marion. Better get this show on the road." At Rudy's words, the front door cowbell announced a patient. Rudy kissed me, hugged Dunham and sprinted back up the walk toward the Gerber house and his medical office. For some reason this made Little Cathie turn handsprings down the sandy alley.

"Let me down. Let me down," Petey yelled but Fermin held his legs tight. "Ella, make him let me down!"

"I can't, Pete. Fermin's a grown-up."

Dunham opened his car door with a sigh and got in. I ran around kissing everyone. This was my stellar moment.

"My baby. My baby." Marion clung to me and I gently tried to squirm loose.

"Oh, for Pete's sake, Marion. I'll bring her down to visit."

"But I'll miss her growing up."

Big Cathie opened my side door and I slipped in and rolled down the window. "Goodbye Barbara, goodbye Lesley, goodbye Petey, goodbye—world." Somehow I couldn't say goodbye to my mother. She took Pete from Fermin and brought him over for a final kiss. Pete and I hung on to each other.

"Oh, Petey, Petey, Petey."

Dunham started the engine. Everyone backed off. I choked up. This was it. I was leaving everyone I had in the world—except Dunham, of course.

"Stand clear, everyone. I'll be in touch, Marion," Dunham called back over his shoulder, easing the car ever so slowly forward. Another moment and they were standing in a semicircle behind us. I twisted around just in time to see everyone head toward the Gerbers' back gate. Big Cathie must have said, "Come on in for coffee and cocoa."

Dunham and I were quiet. I was trying to fix every house, person, stray dog and tree firmly in my mind so I could call them up, one by one, as I went to sleep at night in Berkeley. I was going to have my own bedroom there. The first thing I was going to do was put up photographs of everyone over a whole wall. And some of Edward Weston's photos of the dunes, too.

The next thing I knew we'd crossed Highway One.

"Shouldn't we turn right on Highway One to go north?"

"There's a 9 a.m. low tide and I thought we might take a run down the beach and have a look."

I smiled at my father. How did he know I desperately needed to see the beach again?

We eased onto a spot at the edge of the beach. The tide was way out and there were clammers with pitchforks, the game warden in his grey Plymouth right behind them checking licenses, then making sure every clam was at least five inches long. A dozen pelicans dove for fish in the surf and gulls were underfoot, trying to swipe any broken clam. I wanted to be out there digging too but I sat in the car quietly watching.

I could look down to where the dunes shimmered in the morning sun. If I looked really hard I could even see the pilings two miles down the beach marking the entrance to Moy Mell. Our home.

Dunham put his arm around my shoulder and I snuggled up to him. "Well, Gooch, we're on our own now, you and I, and we have to take care of each other."

"I can wash my clothes and help with dinner."

"And can you go to Sunday matinees and help me pick the good shows for the Screen Writers' Guild Academy Awards?"

"Oh, sure!"

"Okay, I'll help you with homework."

"And I'll learn to make your coffee."

"I like it strong," my father said.

I was happy, so why were these tears rolling down my face?

"Yep, kid, I feel a little like crying myself. It's hell, leaving our life here." My father ruffled my hair as he loosened his arm and turned the key in the ignition. We backed around and headed north on Highway One, six hours away from Berkeley, where we would have our own apartment and there was a school on the corner across the street. My father started to hum and, in a moment, he was singing my favorite chain gang song.

> *Lost one night on a wild horse range, beside a flickering fire,*
> *A coyote came and sat by me and this is what the coyote said:*
> *Don't you know that your hopes are vain?*

I broke in and happily sang along with him. It didn't matter if Carl and my mother said we were monotones and this was a gloomy song. We got the words right and I could hear my coyotes howl. I looked over to find my father grinning at me. Then he wiggled his ears.

I laughed and moved closer to him. "I'm too big for you to wiggle your ears at me anymore," I said.

My dad and I were on our way.

Afterword

WE WERE PULLING OUT OF the Depression by the time Dunham and I reached Berkeley, California, in 1938. We lived in a small apartment across the street from Lincoln Grammar School. I loved school and playing Seabiscuit with the other neighborhood kids. Dunham worked with the WPA but others we knew found jobs in the shipyards and building Treasure Island for the World's Fair.

Dunham was pleased with his editing on *Dune Forum* and felt the magazine had an influence beyond the couple of years it was published. Edward and Brett Weston, Ansel Adams, and Willard Van Dyke got early recognition for their jacket photographs. Langston Hughes, Robinson Jeffers, Helen Hoyt, and Hugo Seelig published poetry. Gavin Arthur, Stewart Edward White, Ella Young, John Cage, and my father wrote stimulating debates and commentary. Thomas Handforth had sent drawings from Peking for *Dune Forum* and went on to win the first Caldecott Award for children's illustration.

Many writers came to Moy Mell to work quietly or read aloud an early chapter or two of their current manuscript. Upton Sinclair started writing again after he lost the race to become the first Democratic governor of California. His work has been translated around the world.

John Steinbeck, who immortalized the Okies in Depression California, visited and read chapters from *Tortilla Flat,* the novel he was working on at the time. He won the Nobel Prize for Literature in 1962.

Spiritual leaders of many faiths, Theosophists, Buddhists, and Hindus, continued to visit. The Sri Meher Baba didn't break his silence for the rest of his life. He stayed mute, using a blackboard and then hand signals, for 44 years. The Baba made several more trips to Hollywood, founded an ashram in North Carolina, but never came back to the dunes. He is an Avatar and his movement thrives today.

Pretty Dolores was still living on the East Coast and she and my father wrote to each other. In 1941, after we'd moved to San Francisco, she came to see Dunham. I was twelve and in junior high school. I hated our dark apartment in the Richmond District. I was enduring periods, head lice, and my first boyfriend. I wanted a mother badly. Pretty Dolores in a leopard skin coat struck me as about perfect. Unfortunately, Dunham was horrified by the leopard skin coat. "Damn coat's bloodthirsty," he said.

Dolores couldn't believe he'd bought matching leather luggage. "Not very Moy Mell," she said with a grin. After a few months, she returned to Washington D.C. where she worked designing books.

War was declared a few months later. One sunny morning, December 7, I was walking home from the bakery and suddenly every radio on the block blared President Roosevelt's voice. "The Japanese are bombing Pearl Harbor. I am asking Congress to declare war," President Roosevelt said.

My father joined the Army in 1942 and soon shipped out for London. I went back to Oceano to live with the Gerbers. My mother still lived across the alley but was slipping further away into catatonia. I wrote about her condition and my struggle to keep her at home in my novel *Celebrate the Morning*.

My six-year-old brother Pete was becoming a juvenile delinquent. He and his friends opened every mailbox in the post office and scattered the town's welfare checks over the floor and sidewalk. They also put rocks on the railroad tracks, once claiming to derail a freight car.

Some of the sand dunes in and near Moy Mell were owned by Gavin Arthur, who turned them over to the Coast Guard in case the Japanese decided to invade. Dunites scattered. Coast Guardsmen and picnickers burned empty shacks for firewood. Doggett got pneumonia and died. Carl married Mary, moved to Pismo, and opened a shell shop. Hugo Seelig moved to a beach trailer court and continued to write poetry. His life there was the background for my novel *Hugo and the Princess Nena*.

Gavin Arthur joined the Merchant Marine. Esther Arthur felt she should be in England doing her part. So did Nannie, my great-grandmother. who had a ship torpedoed under her but made it back to London and survived the war.

Pete in Oceano as a young boy.
Courtesy of Dr. R. W. Gerber Family Papers.

I joined a church in San Luis Obispo where a girlfriend's family went, and there I met and dated V5 Naval Air Cadets and soldiers going overseas. Rudy and Big Cathie didn't want me to date these wild servicemen who were older than me, but I figured it was my life. They warned me that if I continued to misbehave in ways their own children were forbidden to, then I would have to go live with my church friend or my Uncle Godfrey in Washington D.C. I couldn't bear to remember Big Cathie saying their "own children," omitting me, so I just forgot what they said.

Finally, when I got home late one night Rudy said to me, "You are going to end up raped by the side of the road if you continue dating older men. We have girls of our own to look after. You're going to have to stop dating servicemen now if you want to continue living with us."

"How dare you," I yelled, devastated to realize from the sadness on Catherine's face that their girls were still more important than I was to her.

"Dad said I could live with Uncle Godfrey in Washington D.C. if I wanted. So I will."

I marched into Rudy's office, phoned Uncle Godfrey and arranged to live with him and his wife. I left for Washington three days later. This scene of life with the Gerbers was later used in my novel *Sleepwalker's Moon*.

While I lived with my uncle and aunt, my mother was committed to Camarillo State Mental Hospital. She stayed there 28 years, working in the library and playing her record collection for the delight of other patients. The last ten years or so of her hospitalization the doctors thought she was well but she couldn't tolerate the auto and plane noise outside her halfway houses. She always came back to the hospital.

Finally the doctors asked my brother and me to come for a conference. They said many recovering patients were being released and Marion should go as well. If she didn't she would be surrounded by the psychopaths who were left, a dangerous situation.

Our mother said she was used to sleeping in a room with 139 other women. She couldn't live with either my brother or me in a house where she'd be lonely and without worthwhile work. Finally, she agreed to be a nurses' aide in a retirement hospital in San Luis Obispo. As it turned out, she held court in a bowling alley café a block away. Marion's friends from the Moy Mell days came. Her brother moved out from Brooklyn to be near her. Pete and his family lived about a mile away. Marion's old age was happy.

When the State committed our mother to Camarillo Mental Hospital my brother was put in the first of a series of foster homes. Pete liked the singing lessons the welfare department gave him but had a terrible time adjusting to routine, discipline, and loneliness. He didn't see our mother or me again until he was sixteen. In his eyes he'd been abandoned by his family, a viewpoint that was devastating for all three of us. I write about a teenager making his way across the country working in a carnival as he hunts for his only aunt in my novel *Where the Road Ends*.

Pete's father, Jack, had married. My mother claimed he had eleven more children. My brother never met his father or other sisters and brothers. I never saw Jack again after leaving for Washington D.C. However, he would stop by the Gerbers' every few years. Rudy said he still drank heavily. He and Pete, who lived in San Luis Obispo, never met. Fermin Sepulveda moved near Paso Robles with his sister.

Rudy and Catherine Gerber remained in the home they and the Dunites built, welcoming old friends passing through. Rudy treated many of them until he died at ninety. Recently the town of Oceano dedicated a garden to his memory. Catherine became a first rate painter as her girls got older. Two of her daughters also became painters.

At sixteen I caught tuberculosis from my uncle. We thought his coughing came from ulcers. When my father was discharged from the Army he took me out of the Air Force Hospital, brought me back to San Francisco, and put me in Ross General Hospital where, over three years, I recovered from tuberculosis. I tell the story of falling in love with a fellow patient, a Maharajah's son, in *The Year of my Indian Prince*. My father wrote and directed commercial films, some of them prize winners, during this time.

When I was twenty-one I married Leo Ellis, an engineer. We adopted Pete so he could live with us while he went to college. He became a probation officer, married, and had three children.

Leo and I have three sons, nine grandchildren and one great-grandchild. I usually write for young adults but have also written this memoir and am currently working on an adult historical novel. I taught creative writing at San Francisco State University. We've lived in half a dozen countries, including seven years in Argentina, where the adult historical novel and four young adult books are set.

My father married twice more, "each time more unhappily than the last," according to my mother. He finally settled in the Virgin Islands. When I last saw him (after his third marriage broke up) sitting on his deck in St. John, looking out to sea, a glass of scotch by his side, Dunham looked content.

Nearly everyone in this memoir is gone now but it has been a great pleasure to find I could call up beloved voices in these pages.

Wherever I go in the world the cry of a gull overhead or the purr of surf lapping a beach brings happiness. My true home remains in the Oceano dunes facing the Pacific Ocean.

About the Author

Born in the Great Depression, Ella Thorp Ellis grew up in a collective bohemian community on the California coast. Resident artists and writers, including her father and mother, were frequently visited by well-known figures including Upton Sinclair, John Steinbeck, Edward Weston, and Meher Baba. A former lecturer at San Francisco State University, Ella has been celebrated for her young adult novels, six of which were American Library Honor Books of the Year. While Ella made her home for most of her adult life in Berkeley, California, she also lived for many years in Argentina, and for extended periods in Czechoslovakia, Egypt, Jordan, and Russia.

Ella died at home to the sounds of the Pacific surf in Santa Cruz, California, in the fall of 2013. She is survived by her husband of 64 years, three sons, nine grandchildren, and two great-grandchildren.